WITHDRAWN

MODERN NOVELISTS

General Editor: Norman Page

MODERN NOVELISTS

MODERN NOVELISTS

VLADIMIR NABOKOV

David Rampton

St. Martin's Press   New York

First published in the United States of America in 1993

Printed in Hong Kong

ISBN 0–312–09629–1

Library of Congress Cataloging-in-Publication Data
Rampton, David, 1950–
Vladimir Nabokov / David Rampton.
p.   cm. — (Modern novelists)
Includes bibliographical references (p.   ) and index.
ISBN 0–312–09629–1
1. Nabokov, Vladimir Vladimirovich, 1899–1977—Criticism and
interpretation.   I. Title.   II. Series.
PS3527.A15Z88   1993
813'.54—dc20   93–16140
                                                              CIP

Contents

Acknowledgements

I would like to thank A. D. Nuttall and Richard Rorty for their generous responses to my queries about Nabokov's metaphysics, Cedric Watts for helping me discern fifteen long years ago the one thing needful in Nabokov criticism, Grigory Chkhartishvili and Gerald Lynch for their insightful advice, and my wife Elizabeth for her forbearance and numerous helpful suggestions. Thanks also to all the people who have made the English Department at the University of Ottawa such a congenial place to work, to Doreen Alig and Cathryn Tanner at the publishers, and to Tony Grahame for his work as copy-editor.

This book is dedicated to my mother, Florence Rampton, who taught me, among many other things, how to sleep on windy nights.

The author and publishers wish to thank the following who have kindly given permission for the use of copyright material:

The Observer Ltd for an extract from a review of *The Defence* by Stuart Hampshire, *The New Statesman*, 6 November 1964; Weidenfeld and Nicolson Ltd and Random House Inc., New York, for extracts from the works of Vladimir Nabakov – all rights reserved.

Every effort has been made to trace all the copyright-holders but if any have been inadvertently overlooked the publishers will be pleased to make the necessary arrangement at the first opportunity.

General Editor's Preface

The death of the novel has often been announced, and part of the secret of its obstinate vitality must be its capacity for growth, adaptation, self-renewal and self-transformation: like some vigorous organism in a speeded-up Darwinian ecosystem, it adapts itself quickly to a changing world. War and revolution, economic crisis and social change, radically new ideologies such as Marxism and Freudianism, have made this century unprecedented in human history in the speed and extent of change, but the novel has shown an extraordinary capacity to find new forms and techniques and to accommodate new ideas and conceptions of human nature and human experience, and even to take up new positions on the nature of fiction itself.

In the generations immediately preceding and following 1914, the novel underwent a radical redefinition of its nature and possibilities. The present series of monographs is devoted to the novelists who created the modern novel and to those who, in their turn, either continued and extended, or reacted against and rejected, the traditions established during that period of intense exploration and experiment. It includes a number of those who lived and wrote in the nineteenth century but whose innovative contribution to the art of fiction makes it impossible to ignore them in any account of the origins of the modern novel; it also includes the so-called 'modernists' and those who in the mid- and late twentieth century have emerged as outstanding practitioners of this genre. The scope is, inevitably, international; not only, in the migratory and exile-haunted world of our century, do writers refuse to heed national frontiers – 'English' literature lays claim to Conrad the Pole, Henry James the American, and Joyce the Irishman – but geniuses such as Flaubert, Dostoevsky and Kafka have had an influence on the fiction of many nations.

Each volume in the series is intended to provide an introduction to the fiction of the writer concerned, both for those approaching him or her for the first time and for those who are already familiar with some parts of the achievement in question and now wish to place it in the context of the total *oeuvre*. Although essential information relating to the writer's life and times is given, usually in an opening chapter, the approach is primarily critical and the emphasis is not upon 'background' or generalisations but upon close examination of important texts. Where an author is notably prolific, major texts have been made to convey, more summarily, a sense of the nature and quality of the author's work as a whole. Those who want to read further will find suggestions in the select bibliography included in each volume. Many novelists are, of course, not only novelists but also poets, essayists, biographers, dramatists, travel writers and so forth; many have practised shorter forms of fiction; and many have written letters or kept diaries that constitute a significant part of their literary output. A brief study cannot hope to deal with all these in detail, but where the shorter fiction and the non-fictional writings, public and private, have an important relationship to the novels, some space has been devoted to them.

NORMAN PAGE

1

Introduction

In Russian, 'Vladimir' rhymes with 'redeemer' and 'Nabokov' with 'the gawk of',[1] but deciding where the accent should fall in assessing the novels of this supremely talented Russian-American writer is a somewhat more difficult task. For one thing, his supranational status has been a problem for those attempting to locate him on the literary map. Definitions of contemporary literature as the product of an international or at least a postnational consciousness have proved premature, and the most striking political truth of recent times – that nationalism is still at least as potent a force as any single political ideology – finds its literary counterpart in the refusal of the novel to transcend all the limitations imposed upon it by language and culture.

Born in Russia on 23 April 1899, forced to flee with his family after the Bolshevik coup in 1917 (his father was a liberal statesman who served in Kerensky's provisional government), Nabokov began his career as 'Vladimir Sirin', a Russian *émigré* novelist, that is, as a writer with only a portable culture and a series of literary reference points to constitute home and audience, and the world of *émigré* letters is still more or less unknown to the reading public in the West. Some of Nobel prize-winner Ivan Bunin's stories are occasionally anthologized. Thanks to course requirements in university Slavic departments, Alexey Remizov's work is still available, as are novels by Adamovich, Aldanov, and Gazdanov, but these authors tend to gather a lot of dust on library shelves, if they have not disappeared to the storage room altogether. *Émigré* poets, though harder to translate, have done a little better, but the number of readers who regularly curl up with, say, Marina Tsvetaeva, the best of a talented group, might fill an Intourist bus or two, but would be lost in the expanses of Red Square. The level of interest in the work of their Soviet contemporaries, writers like Vladimir Mayakovsky,

Maxim Gorky, and Osip Mandelstam, suggests that the literature of Soviet Russia still has an appeal for Western readers, in a way that *émigré* literature does not.

If the emigration does not provide much of a context for Nabokov because in the minds of most readers he *is* the emigration, attempts to locate him in relation to his nineteenth-century forebears have proved equally inconclusive. Either the figures are too immense, Tolstoy, for example, to be anything more than a general 'runs-in-the-blood-of-all-Russian-writers' type of influence. Or they are, like Dostoevsky and Chekhov, on the surface too different from Nabokov, and their range of fictional interests, prose style, attachment to their own time and place make it difficult for us to see the links. The quintessentially Russian interest in 'love and the soul and human progress'[2] in such novelists makes their work feel different. Other nineteenth-century Russian writers, such as Goncharov, Turgenev, Leskov, and Saltykov-Shchedrin, with their commitment to public concerns, their willingness to serve as the political and social conscience of a nation, seem equally unrelated to Nabokov's aesthetic stance and practice.

Of course Nabokov was also an American writer, who came to the United States in 1940, taught at Wellesley and Cornell for almost twenty years, and wrote eight of his seventeen novels in English. Like J. D. Salinger and Philip Roth, he burst onto the literary scene with a single novel, *Lolita*, and became irrevocably identified in the public mind with it. He loved his new country and the intellectual freedom it had to offer, but did he ever become 'as American as April in Arizona',[3] as he liked to claim? Clearly not, in the sense that Dreiser or Fitzgerald, Dos Passos or Sinclair Lewis were; that is, he did not write about peculiarly American aspirations or about the circumstances that conspire to confound them. Nor were his books systematically grounded in a contemporary American reality, as were those of Bellow, Mailer or Updike, to name three very different writers from the next generation. Even those with fictional interests similar to Nabokov's seem American in a way that he does not. Robert Coover locates his fantasy *The Public Burning* in the Eisenhower era and retells the story of the execution of the Rosenbergs for espionage; Thomas Pynchon re-creates the world of California dreams and nightmares in *The Crying of Lot 49* and *Vineland*; and John Barth, one of America's most talented experimental novelists, began his career writing about a young man in Dorchester County,

Maryland, where he was brought up, and has located two of his most recent novels, replete with their quintessentially American critiques of the CIA, in the same location. And, typically, all of these writers are preoccupied in their work with political power and the sources from which it flows in a way that Nabokov manifestly is not.

Even if one forgoes the quest for a precise national designation, Nabokov resists categorization in other ways as well. The experimental nature of the great modernist fiction written in the first three decades of the century, its preoccupation with consciousness, introspection, reverie, its tendency to leave endings open and problematic, its emphasis on new modes of aesthetic ordering as narrative unity becomes less important, its play with multiple viewpoints and its complex handling of time, constitutes one tradition that Nabokov inherits and extends. He was, by his own admission, a product of the period in pre-revolutionary Russia during which Russian literature was modernized by experimental poets like the Symbolists and Acmeists, and he read widely in English literature from an early age, including Joyce's *Ulysses* soon after its publication in 1922. But his novels sometimes seem like the work of a reluctant or partially committed modernist. Nabokov affords us glimpses across the boundaries of conventional morality, but unlike, say, Conrad or Mann, he often stops short of requiring us to question fundamental assumptions about the ethical norms that inform our culture. He is as intrigued by the limits of rationality as Lawrence or Musil or Unamuno, but unlike them he is relatively uninterested in exploring the radical reordering of human relations that might result from a new way of seeing the interaction between reason and emotion. Nabokov's work has singular affinities with Kafka's, and his heroes often find themselves poised between an affirmation of the world and an urge to transcend it, but the systemic ambiguity that characterizes Kafka's work functions much more fitfully and less threateningly in Nabokov's. His lexical and syntactic experiments, narrative patterning, and stylistic innovation often rival those of Bely and Joyce. But Bely's *Petersburg* is the great symbolist novel *and* a study of the revolutionary consciousness, Joyce's *Ulysses* one of the most dazzling feats of technical virtuosity ever attempted by a writer *and* a cross section of a whole city at a given moment in time. What has been perceived as the circumscribed nature of Nabokov's material and the relatively limited range of his fictional interests has tended to limit the appeal of his experiments.

Nabokov's position *vis-à-vis* postmodernism constitutes yet another reason for his curiously indeterminate status. After the success of *Lolita*, Nabokov gave up teaching and moved to Montreux, Switzerland (he died there in 1977), where he published some brilliantly innovative novels that gained him a reputation as the *éminence grise* of postmodernist fiction. Suggestions that Beckett and Borges were his real *confrères* were popular for a while, but as Nabokov himself put it, given the veneration with which those two figures are regarded, linked with them he would feel like 'a robber between two Christs. Quite a cheerful robber, though'.[4] There are still those who consider him part of a movement which sees the novel as moribund and its conventions as both spurious and presumptuous. Forced to live in a world that has moved beyond the shared assumptions that legitimized the realists' enterprise, we (so the argument runs) have jettisoned the assurance, the cosiness of the bourgeois world view with which they are associated, and by which they are deeply compromised, and managed to come to terms with a new form of fiction for a new, post-humanist world. Yet Nabokov's persistent reliance on certain realistic techniques, his defence of values that he regards as trans-historical and trans-cultural, and the broadly humanist assumptions about self and world implicit in much of his work make him at best only a part-time ally for Donald Barthelme and Michel Butor, Italo Calvino and Sasha Sokolov. Nabokov's postmodernist impersonality (parody, foregrounding of devices) is repeatedly juxtaposed with the old-fashioned 'personality' that makes the novels so distinctively his. In fiction that formally acknowledges just how ideologically grounded any literary representation is, he openly mocks the relevance of ideology to any kind of critical inquiry.

A more accommodating view of postmodernism would contend that the novel has continued to circle around an emotive centre, to speak about human values, to concern itself with psychology, to trace and comment upon man's evolving fate in history; or at least that novelists are right to proceed on the assumption that such an enterprise is still possible. Though Nabokov could more easily be included in any group thus described, so too could Anita Brookner, Philip Roth, and Alexander Solzhenitsyn. The less grimly exclusive view better reflects the multiplicity of the current state of fictional affairs, but if we adopt it we may lose our sense of what makes postmodernism genuinely distinctive.

Many of Nabokov's critics feel that the very idea of classifying and comparing this unique author is a misguided exercise, that his repugnance for critical generalizations should exempt him from such categorization. But, as Richard Rorty points out, 'no individual achievement of importance escapes such banalization, because "importance" is determined precisely by the degree of effort it takes to bring the particular under the universal, to synthesize the idiosyncratic with the social. The most important achievements are those which make such a synthesis extraordinarily difficult while nevertheless not making it impossible'.[5]

A final curiosity of Nabokov's reputation is its doubly disjunctive quality: in North America and most of Western Europe he is extravagantly praised, enormously admired by a very dedicated readership inside *and* outside the university, but for many literate people he is still the obscure author of one phenomenal bestseller. Although Nabokov has always been read by lovers of literature in Russia, the large-scale publishing of his work there in recent years has made him a tremendous number of new fans, but even in his native country critics are divided about the nature of his achievement. In addition to the reasons cited above, the multilingual puns, literary allusions, and general self-reflexiveness of his late novels have made readers dismiss them as destined for a coterie only. There are no doubt many who enjoy Nabokov precisely because he does not write for just anyone, and some books about him have the air of being written to be passed around among a small group of knowing admirers. But authorial comments in interviews like 'I write for myself in multiplicate',[6] disparaging references to readers who like to identify with the characters and move their lips while reading, merely confirmed for many the feeling that Nabokov is not only somewhat inaccessible (many twentieth-century writers are that) but that he is also wilfully and unrewardingly so.

Because Nabokov's work has evoked such a variety of response, those who write about him have sometimes tended to adopt a defensive tone in characterizing his achievements. His own contributions to discussions of his work were both delightfully and magisterially phrased: Nabokov once subjected a Festschrift put together as a tribute to his genius to an article-by-article analysis, in which he graciously acknowledged the praise but also corrected misstatements, disputed interpretations, and generally tidied up the views professed by his admirers. His idiosyncratic notions about subjects as various as perception, immortality, and literary merit, his insistence on the importance of hidden patterns and deception, his views on the fairytale essence of seemingly realistic fiction, his

contempt for the journalistic vacuity of all socially relevant literature, the 'strong opinions' that made him such a good interview,
distilled from ideas worked out in detail in the lectures he gave at
Wellesley and Cornell in the 1940s and 1950s – these have helped
determine the directions taken by the criticism of his novels. Since
so many perceptive studies have been written about Nabokov from
the point of view of what he thought he was trying to do, in this
study I have tried to suggest how the novels might be seen from a
variety of critical perspectives. The literature on his work is so vast
– the books, articles and dissertations devoted to it now number
more than a thousand – that any brief introductory book about
him threatens to turn into a 'frozen frenzy of footnotes' (Nabokov's
phrase) if certain limits are not determined from the outset. I have
therefore kept indications of my indebtedness to a minimum, and
I take pleasure in acknowledging here what I owe to the many
critics whose works have been so helpful, both as information and
provocation. Exigencies of space also required me to omit any
discussion of *King, Queen, Knave* and *Pnin,* two of Nabokov's more
straightforward novels, and *Transparent Things,* which I consider
to be among his less interesting. Since the traditional distinction
between general reader and specialist critic is particularly marked
in the case of Nabokov's fiction, I have concentrated in this book on
providing a reading guide for the former, while trying to address at
various points the concerns of the latter.

   In the conclusions to many of his books, Nabokov, like all
great comic writers, invites his readers to share in the essential
strangeness of the storyteller's art, that power that takes us into a
world where nothing is certain except that we must leave it. Then
he eases us out of it, purged of certainty, and into its inscrutable,
intriguing counterpart which we rediscover as our own. What
should emerge in this study is a portrait of a writer who is this
kind of serious comedian, and whose subject is ultimately ourselves:
our yearning to know, to experience, to create, and our encounters
with a mysterious reality that mockingly rewards us with a sort of
success.

2
Lives of a Young *Émigré*: *Mary*, *Glory*, and *The Gift*

Mary, *Glory*, and *The Gift*, novels taken from the beginning, middle and end of the fifteen-year period during which Nabokov wrote his Russian novels, all depict a young man's coming of age. They provide a particularly appropriate introduction to Nabokov's work because they focus on so many of his central concerns, and because the autobiographical elements in them give them a special status in his *oeuvre*.

Mary (1925) tells the story of Lev Ganin, a young Russian *émigré* in Berlin whose life is poised between the past and the future. About to leave a woman he no longer cares about and a country in which he feels alienated, he discovers that the great love of his youth, Mary, now the wife of fellow lodger, is coming to Berlin. His detailed reveries about her help him transcend his sordid present, a boarding house filled with a group of *émigrés* who are a lost generation (not just playing at being one like their American counterparts in Paris), and he decides to recover the past by intercepting Mary at the train station when she arrives and taking her away with him. At the last moment, he changes his mind and leaves Germany for the south of France, alone, in search of new adventures.

The strengths of the novel are twofold: the meticulous delineation of the sights and sounds of *émigré* Berlin, and the evocation of Ganin's Russian past, his life with Mary. For both, Nabokov has drawn heavily on his own past, and many of the passages about Russia are paralleled in *Speak, Memory*, his autobiography. Though *Mary* offers little in the way of formal innovation, it retains an important place in Nabokov's work as an interesting contribution

to the tradition of the *Bildungsroman*, the first of a triumvirate of
novels that plot the youth and maturation of a young man, and as
an example of 'the road not taken', the relatively straightforward
novel of character and incident that Nabokov would eschew for the
rest of his career.

Consider the following passage in which the narrative brings
Ganin's reveries into sharp focus for the first time:

> He was a god, re-creating a world that had perished. Gradually
> he resurrected that world, to please the girl whom he did not
> dare to place in it until it was absolutely complete. But her image,
> her presence, the shadow of her memory demanded that in the
> end he must resurrect her too – and he intentionally thrust away
> her image, as he wanted to approach it gradually, step by step,
> just as he had done nine years before. (37/33)

The Nabokov hero in love almost always proceeds in this fashion,
reinventing the object of his affection for a sort of solipsistic
delectation. Here, of course, Ganin is conjuring up memories, but
even before meeting his Mary, he has in effect dreamed her into
being:

> The fact was that he had been waiting for her with such longing,
> had thought so much about her during those blissful days after
> the typhus, that he had fashioned her unique image long before
> he actually saw her. Now, many years later, he felt that their
> imaginary meeting and the meeting which took place in reality
> had blended and merged imperceptibly into one another, since
> as a living person she was only an uninterrupted continuation of
> the image which had foreshadowed her. (46/44)

It is simply a given in the novels that the really significant affairs
between the male heroes and the women they seek begin and
end in this kind of elaborate fatality and image-making. Thus in
Nabokov's first love story, the girl herself never appears, except as
a creation of memory. Ganin is exclusively motivated by his own
feelings, even at the end when he rejects the idea of a reunion
with Mary, but Nabokov has no earnest moral point to make about
youthful egotism. In his later novels he would carefully delineate
just how easily romantic preoccupation with the self could lead to
a narcissistic self-absorption with disastrous consequences for those

whose lives are linked with the hero's. But *Mary* celebrates Ganin's independent maturity, and its ending constitutes his recognition that such passion is specific to a time and place, that there will be other passions, equally intense and perhaps more durable, and that if he is to be true to the impulse that made him 'create' Mary in the first place, he must not attempt to re-create her; that story is finished. Mary can also enjoy only a part-time existence in the novel because she is busy doing double-duty as a symbol of Ganin's Russian past, and Nabokov's. He says in the Introduction '[Ganin's] Mary is a twin sister of my Tamara [in *Speak, Memory*], the Oredezh flows through both books, and the actual photograph of the Rozhestveno house as it is today . . . could well be a picture of the pillared porch in the "Voskresensk" of the novel'.[1] The Russia actually re-created in the novel seems, like the one in all those pre-revolutionary photograph albums, hauntingly evocative and a trifle unreal. It is very sparsely populated – only Mary exists in it – and obviously the private preserve of the aristocrat. (Visiting the Nabokov family home in St Petersburg and the house on his uncle's country estate gives one a sense of how luxurious life was for people of Nabokov's class in Russia at the beginning of this century.)

The other theme that was to preoccupy Nabokov throughout his fiction is touched on in this early novel as well, bound up as it is with the notions of fictional creation and nostalgia. Musing about his past life in Russia, Ganin thinks:

> And where is it all now? . . . Where is the happiness, the sun-shine, where are those thick skittles of wood which crashed and bounced so nicely, where is my bicycle with the low handlebars and the big gear? It seems there's a law which says that nothing ever vanishes, that matter is indestructible; therefore the chips from my skittles and the spokes of my bicycle still exist some-where to this day. The pity of it is that I'll never find them again – never. I once read about the 'eternal return'. But what if this complicated game of patience never comes out a second time? Let me see – there's something I don't grasp – yes, this: surely it won't all die when I do? (38/34)

Nostalgia is always object-specific in Nabokov, and his heroes are repeatedly bemused by the fact that the past can be utterly gone, when they have such vivid images of the things that inhabited it.

The phrase in inverted commas suggests that Ganin has been reading German philosophy, but his youthful preoccupation with self
has prevented him from understanding the point at issue. Nietzsche
says that since the universe cannot infinitely renew itself it must infinitely repeat itself, and that this produces eternal monotony, with
the compensation that man must forget about 'life's goal', 'higher
states', and similar metaphysical abstractions. And Nietzsche does
not associate this with anything as concrete as childhood toys, or
the idea of intentionality, quite the contrary: his eternal return
is bound up with his sense of a new scientific spirit that opposes
itself to old beliefs in a controlling force like a Deity. What Ganin
has responded to in Nietzsche's work is more generalized, the
challenge to 'stamp the form of eternity on our lives' because they
are eternal, properly understood.[2]

In many of the poems he wrote in the 1920s Nabokov indulges
in similar musings about first and last things, and *Mary* echoes
them. At one point Ganin sees each passer-by as 'a wholly isolated world, each a totality of marvels and evil', and concludes
that 'It is at moments like this that everything grows fabulous,
unfathomably profound, when life seems terrifying and death even
worse'(31–32/27). Such passages are somewhat crude early versions of the meditations that occur throughout Nabokov's fiction,
musings about the fundamental strangeness of what it means to be
a human being, that odd congeries of memories and impressions
bundled into a isolated entity that swirls through time towards
death. One of the ways in which he developed as a novelist was
learning that the attempt to conceptualize such questions often
results in earnest banalities. The mysterious would have to inhere
in the structure of the novels themselves if it was to be successfully
recreated.

Ganin's problems with such large questions are finally problems
with language, and he slowly comes to understand that the very
nature of his past experiences will be affected by the way in which
he articulates them. At one point he tells an old poet about his
amorous adventures in the country and his interlocutor says: '"I
can see it all. Rather hackneyed, though. Sweet sixteen, love in
the woods."' Ganin is puzzled by this response and replies '"But
what could be nicer?"' (44/42) The implication is that maturity
will give Ganin the self-awareness he lacks here, the ability to see
even the genuine experiences he remembers as potential clichés, if
they are not fashioned in a language that makes them memorable.

In *Speak, Memory*, Nabokov remarks that as a youth engaged in the simultaneous balancing of multilevel impressions, he was 'serenely aware of [his] own manifold awareness'.[3] Ganin's consciousness features the ethereal interweaving of richly annotated memories and sensory reactions, but he has not yet attained this extra dimension which will be granted to Fyodor in *The Gift*, the most Nabokov-like hero in these early, partly autobiographical, novels.

In *Glory*, the country and the cast of characters are different, but the focus is basically the same: how does a young man deal with the special problems created by exile, what course is his life to take now as he reconciles himself to adulthood? Named this time Martin Edelweiss, Nabokov's protagonist is given chunks of his creator's life just as Ganin was. Like Nabokov, Martin escapes from the Crimea during the Civil War and goes to London via Turkey and Greece, attends Cambridge, and ends up in Berlin, and the scenes that take place in these locales constitute by far the most memorable parts of the book. Nabokov remarks in the Foreword that readers would be ill-advised to search out passages in *Speak, Memory* that recount the scenes and events found in *Glory*, not because the parallels are not there but because his rigorously impersonal stance as author is somewhat compromised by all this self-borrowing. In any event, the plot in which Martin is involved sufficiently distances him from his creator. Feeling the need to demonstrate his courage by risking his personal safety, Nabokov's hero plans to enter the Soviet Union illegally and return. Like Ganin, he fantasizes about joining the cause of the counter-revolutionaries, but ultimately the reasons for his 'high deed' (a literal translation of *Podvig*, the book's Russian title) are as private and personal as Ganin's.

Like Ganin, Martin Edelweiss also tends to cast himself in the rôle of romantic hero: the talented individual who rebels against social and religious convention, establishes his own set of values based on the intensity of individual experiences, seeks out such experiences in awe-inspiring Nature, and makes his lonely way towards the high ideal he has set himself, but must function in the ordinary world where such quests are often doubted, misunderstood or thwarted.[4] He flouts the conventional expectations of friends and relatives by committing himself to his quixotic venture. Nabokov stresses the utter uselessness of the act to underline just how uncommitted his hero is to any kind of political gesture, which makes him a rebel without a cause, setting himself arbitrarily a dangerous task so that he can prove his courage to himself. Martin sets about creating his own set of values as well. The religion of his youth also seems to have made only a slight, purely aesthetic impression upon him. His mother conceives of God as a sort of absentee landlord, but although Martin tries with 'the full force of his soul' (18/11) to find evidence of an afterlife, he gets nowhere. It is only when he gives himself up to the world whose presence is constantly hinted at in the novel, a world that his dreams lead him towards and that can be entered by the transposition of realms that might take place if he can 'think' himself into the painting above his bed and walk down its twisting path into the forest – only then does he get close to the spiritual realms whose existence he is gifted enough to intuit. We learn that in the end Martin has done precisely this, vanished by taking a similar path into his old country, and he dies into the book as a result. Again, just what this means is wide open to various conjectures. In recent years critics have argued that such an adventure is a manifestation of *the* Nabokov theme: 'What lies beyond death may be the main text to which life is only a preface: because at death one's life may be read backward or forward, in any order at all, so that this timeless version of one's life itself becomes the main text, unreachable in mortal time, that allows the unique design of one's life to show through'.[5] As Nabokov knows perfectly well, it is equally likely that one will discover that the whole of the universe is propped up on the back of a giant turtle: speculations in this area have all the attractions *and* all the limitations that the products of the unconstrained imagination always have. But the notion of a 'unique design' that 'shows through' at epiphanic moments is a crucially important theme in Nabokov's novels.

The other romantic traits on the list included above are also exemplified by young Martin. Nature in her wilder, more awe-inspiring aspects figures prominently in all his confrontations with danger or the unknown. Just before leaving the Crimea, Martin stands on the edge of a precipice, and has the first of a series of quintessentially romantic experiences:

> above the black alpestrine steppe ['Yayla mountains' in *Podvig*], above the silken sea, the enormous, all-engulfing sky, dove-gray with stars, made one's head spin, and suddenly Martin again experienced a feeling he had known on more than one occasion as a child: an unbearable intensification of all his senses, a magical and demanding impulse, the presence of something for which alone it was worth living. (28/20)

His first encounter with death, in the form of a drunk who threatens to shoot him, occurs in similarly evocative surroundings. The second occurs while climbing in the Swiss mountains, when he slips and lands on a cornice:

> His ledge recalled the stage setting of nightmares. . . . With an effort glancing over his shoulder, he saw under his heels a prodigious precipice, a sun-illumined abyss with, in its depths, several outdistanced firs running in panic after the descending forest, and still further down the steep meadows and the tiny, ivory white hotel. (101/85)

The comic trope ('firs running in panic') both vivifies the description and gently undercuts the romantic grandeur of the scene, but he interprets the encounter as a important 'message' from the natural world, a message about courage and risking death. Irritated by his own fear, he returns to the scene in the mountains to master it, and again it is precisely the wild quality of the natural surroundings that Nabokov chooses to emphasize. This time Martin forces himself to smoke a cigarette while he stands on the ledge, feeling all the time 'the abyss behind him strain and pull at his calves and shoulders'; the 'absolute noiselessness' of a falling object is 'awesome' (195/169). In the final scene, when Darwin goes to inform Martin's mother that her son is missing, he finds himself in a landscape that eerily recapitulates the one in the picture hanging above Martin's bed when he was a child, the scene which presumably confronts Martin when he crosses the border, 'the dark path [that] passed between the tree trunks in picturesque and mysterious windings' (235/205). The parallels in English literature are Wordsworth and Byron (via Pushkin), the former for his evocation of those moments when he realizes that the harmony he perceives in nature speaks so directly to him because it is his part in that harmony that enables him to perceive it, the latter for his lonely, cloaked, wandering heroes in precipitous circumstances who perform deeds of valour commensurate with the grandeur of the scenes in which they moodily muse about performing such deeds.

The typical Romantic conflict between the transcendent and the mundane, and the consequent tension between a desire for solitude and a desire for community manifest themselves in the lives of many of Nabokov's characters as well. In *Glory* we have

Martin the loner, the soccer goalie at Cambridge who exults in his solitary and unique responsibility, Martin the lonely dreamer, the isolated expatriate, the explorer of remote regions. Dreams send him important signals from the beyond that continually haunts him, as they do so many figures in Romantic literature, and confirm his sense that the private search for intensity of experience is all that ultimately matters. His extraordinarily vivid awareness of his own uniqueness enables him to know his dreams will come true. But the novel is full of the concerns of this world as well: Martin ingratiates himself with a family in London who puts him up, worries about what his mother will think, gets into trouble pursuing mercenary women, joins a group of Russian *émigrés* at university, and generally spends a considerable amount of time concerned about what kind of impression he is making.

Martin's years at Cambridge are the ostensible centre of the novel. This part has been dismissed, somewhat harshly, as 'post-cards and Rupert Brooke', yet there is a sense in which the intense introspection always lurking in a Nabokov novel does dominate over the portrait of university life. Here is a typical passage:

> Beauty dwells in the light and stillness of laboratories: like an expert diver gliding through the water with open eyes, the biologist gazes with relaxed eyelids into the microscope's depths, and his neck and forehead slowly begin to flush, and, tearing himself away from the eyepiece, he says, 'That settles everything'. Human thought, flying on the trapezes of the star-filled universe, with mathematics stretched beneath, was like an acrobat working with a net but suddenly noticing that in reality there is no net, and Martin envied those who attained that vertigo and, with a new calculation, overcame their fear. Predicting an element or creating a theory, discovering a mountain chain or naming a new animal, were all equally enticing. (74/61–2)

This is Martin trying to choose a field of study, and Nabokov has admirably conveyed the young student's eclectic enthusiasms, the 'Eureka!' view of scientific inquiry that characterizes neophytes and non-scientists generally, and the charming naïveté implied by the assumption that taking an undergraduate degree in any one of these subjects will one day lead the degree holder to an astounding breakthrough. Yet by having Martin opt for Russian as his course of study, Nabokov denies himself the chance of exploiting this naïveté.

Instead he uses the choice to explore again the whole question of the appropriate attitude for the expatriate. Quite clearly the wrong answer is to assume that Russia is dead, and can now be preserved in a sort of aestheticized amber for the delectation of aficionados, the attitude of one of Martin's Russian tutors who is writing a book on this moribund country. The answer that Nabokov will propose in *The Gift* is that Russia lives on in its literature, that the only genuine return for the writer is 'with pen in hand'. For now, he can let Martin's general interest hint at the direction in which a possible answer might lie. This keeps his involvement as a student at the strictly notional level: seminars, lectures, papers, exams, the whole business side of a student's life is almost totally ignored. In its place there are charming vignettes: a soccer game, a sexual conquest that creates complications for earnest young Martin when the girl pretends she's pregnant, a fist-fight with his best friend over a question of honour. These are hardly postcards. True, they don't take us very far into the world of a Cambridge student in the early 1920s, but Nabokov's objections to generalities made him refuse to the credit the existence of such a world.[6]

Nabokov dismissed this early work as *blevotina* (vomit),[7] probably because the courage and daring of the hero, who is systematically portrayed as admirable, is compromised by an essential silliness in the plot. The need to remain aloof, to keep the deed *inutile*, is something Nabokov felt strongly, but few readers will understand why. So the ending, Martin's apparently pointless death, becomes something of a problem, even when the presence of 'the otherworld' is there to explain it. Some have argued for a carefully delineated irony that exposes the selfishness of Martin's final act. If there is such an irony, we the readers are implicated by it as well. Reading Nabokov's fiction, our moralizing expectations are constantly being challenged and confounded by our yearning for imaginative excitement: part of us hopes that Ganin and Martin will achieve their fondest desires, even if this means emptiness and loss for the people left behind. No writer who explores so attentively, so convincingly, the mentality of the self-styled romantic hero should be read as systematically espousing the values of the community that hero sometimes scorns.

The Gift begins with a Foreword in which Nabokov once again warns readers not to identify him with the hero of the novel, this time Count Fyodor Godunov-Cherdyntsev. Nabokov cites some obvious differences between himself and his creation: he notes that he had a different father, different girlfriend, different attitude to his fellow writers, and adds that other characters in the novel have some of his traits as well. This list of disclaimers need not detain us long. True, Nabokov's father, a man with a profound interest in helping Russia solve its social and political problems, was not an explorer in Central Asia, but a mere change of occupation cannot disguise the fact he is enormously present in *The Gift*, as a model of valour and aristocratic honour, if not as a collection of facts. Zina Mertz, like the late Véra Nabokov, acts as friend, companion, muse, and sympathetic audience for the male around whom her life circles, but she is such a shadowy figure in the novel that the resemblance is more or less inconsequential. As for which of *The Gift*'s panoply of writers most resembles its creator, the crucial passage is the following (one Vladimirov is being described):

> his eyes looked out with intelligence and indifference – he had studied, it seemed, at an English university and flaunted a pseudo-British manner. At twenty-nine he was already the author of two novels – outstanding for the force and swiftness of their mirror-like style – which irritated Fyodor perhaps for the very reason he felt a certain affinity with him. As a conversationalist Vladimirov was singularly unattractive. One blamed him for being derisive, supercilious, cold, incapable of thawing to friendly discussions – but that was also said about Koncheyev and about Fyodor himself, and about anyone whose thoughts lived in their own private house and not in a barrack-room or a pub. (359/333)

Here is certainly the most likely candidate for the Nabokov stand-in in the novel, but the last sentence says everything the reader needs to know about how the writers in *The Gift* divide up. There is the Nabokov type, the loner who knows or will learn that popularity must finally be a matter of perfect indifference to him, like the world of fleshly desires for a monk, and there are all the rest, those who crave group recognition and club together to disguise their own mediocrity. This is probably the single most important fact about Nabokov's presentation of himself as a writer. It informs his way of seeing the world and its human artefacts. He alludes to it in interview after interview, and whenever he figures in his novels he displays the same quasi-contemptuous confidence in his own enormous ability, and his sense that such ability always defines

itself *against* the mediocrity of others. Chekhov once noted that
what the aristocrat takes for granted, the rest of us must pay for
with our youth. *The Gift* is the novel in which Nabokov explores
in most detail the development of this feeling of superiority in a
young man who is an aristocrat by birth and by virtue of his special
talent.

It is also a novel that lends itself particularly well to comparisons
with the other *künstlerromane* that so many modern masters tried
their hand at during the first part of this century. In the Foreword
Nabokov describes the novel as the chronicle of Fyodor's coming
of age as a writer. There is, Nabokov claims, a literary subject
at the heart of each chapter, and the 'heroine' of the book
is 'Russian literature'. In what follows I shall attempt to make
sense of these claims, by showing how a novel that gives only
an oblique and subjective account of the life of its 'heroine', as
part of a collection of impressions organized around three years
of a young *émigré*'s life in Berlin in the 1920s, actually becomes
Nabokov's most interesting description of the writer's life as he
chose to lead it.

The title denotes the special talent that Fyodor and figures like
Koncheyev and Vladimirov possess. The epigraph, taken from a
handbook of Russian grammar, reminds us that this 'gift', this
private phenomenon, manifests itself in something public, in language: 'An oak is a tree. A rose is a flower. A deer is an animal.
A sparrow is a bird. Russia is our fatherland. Death is inevitable'
(9/15). Lists of sentences like these have taken generations of
Russian students through an elementary taxonomy that begins with
the organization of the natural world into individuals and species,
and ends with a biological fact that reminds us of the difference
between individuals and species. The patriotic note sounded in the
midst of the list serves as an anachronistic reminder that this book
by and about a Russian exile will focus on what time does to other
categories, which are none the less as timeless in their own way
as grammar and biology. In Russian the verb 'to be' in sentences
where both subject and predicate are single nouns is replaced
by a dash ('Oak – tree' etc.), giving an equal status to both.
This dash disappears in the last sentence, with its noun/adjective
construction, marking the phenomenon recorded in it as different
in kind. That is, the inevitability of death is not simply one of its
attributes, but something closer, more intimate. The taxonomic
propositions help us organize the world's raw material; the one

about death would seem to be equally unexceptionable, but it is a more problematic claim because it occurs in a novel in which memory seeks to re-create the past and deny the crass truth asserted so blankly here.

As Chapter One opens, Fyodor's sense of his manifest destiny as a writer is confirmed by the news that an extremely laudatory review of his recently published book of poems has appeared. Impatiently anticipating the pleasure of reading it, Fyodor rereads his book, and comments on the strengths and weaknesses of his verse. When the 'review' turns out to be an April Fool joke played on him by his friend Alexander Chernyshevsky, Fyodor's account of the poems has already superseded it. This is the first of a number of instances that reveal Nabokov's subject to be the intense, inner world of his hero, that invulnerable self-sufficiency granted him by his creative imagination, his gift.

The tutelary spirit of Fyodor's poetry is Alexander Pushkin (1799–1837), who dominates Russian verse the way Shakespeare does English drama, but is even more genuinely popular, if the ability of Russian cabdrivers to quote and comment upon poetry is a reliable index. He is also Russia's greatest poet but not its most Russian poet,[8] a characteristic of particular importance to a young poet looking to forge his identity as an expatriate. His pivotal role in the creation of Russian literature, his passionate defence of liberty, his stylistic purity – all these make him the ideal guide for the young *émigré* writer as well. Pushkin worked successfully in just about every literary genre, but in *The Gift* Nabokov is most interested in Pushkin the lyricist. He was a master of the poem as keepsake, a love poem in which the speaker muses on prospective views of the present: 'On some sad day, in the silence, pronounce my name with yearning', that kind of thing. Such poems are quite clearly the product of an upper-class culture in which one has the time and the inclination for such musings, a culture guided by the eighteenth-century notions of decorum still current in Pushkin's day, but in them he gave a new literary status to the language of ordinary speech as well. Nabokov updates the language and the concerns of such poems in some of Fyodor's early verse, as a kind of homage to Russia's premier poet and a triple link with the past, Fyodor's, his own (some of the incidents in the first chapter are reproduced in his autobiography), and Russian literature's. The other side of Pushkin's work that Nabokov particularly responds to presents the poet as heroic figure, the epitome of the freedom-loving *isolato* who dreams of lonely exile even while in Russia, the champion of artistic freedom who liked to insist 'The aim of poetry is poetry', although Pushkin also regarded poetry as the means of speaking to and for a nation, a medium for fiery prophecy and an inspirer of kindly sentiments. The great lyric tradition extends through major figures like Tyutchev and Fet and through some of the minor ones whom Nabokov sometimes seems to be imitating, like Vladimir Benediktov, and culminates in the verse of the Symbolists.

As Fyodor revises his poems, we realize that, for all the quiet competence they demonstrate and the minute particulars they provide, they are not the primary thing. Rather Nabokov wants to use this 'reading' to incorporate the details of early childhood and youth which are always of such importance for his heroes. As in *Mary* and *Glory*, the aristocratic background of the hero conditions most of the ways in which he will see the world as an adult. Once again, the privileged world of servants and *noblesse oblige* gives the whole of Chapter One the 'preserved' aura of the pre-Revolutionary photo album whose fascination is bound up with the imminent disappearance of the scenes it contains. The quasi-magical, protected quality of this world enables the Nabokov hero to cope, because it forces him to believe that if life was once that dream-like, then surely it can be again. (In a letter to Edmund Wilson, Nabokov, discussing the use of the instrumental case in Russian with the past tense of the verb 'to be', a construction that can also suggest an impossible condition, insists that 'to have been a boy is as fantastic as the dream of being some day a rich old man').[9] He, like his creator, can put up with hardship because his childhood has given him such a secure sense of self.

The risk of such evocations is always self-indulgent sentimentality. Nabokov cleverly avoids this by blaming his imaginary reviewer for trying to turn the poems into mere sentimental evocations:

> Again something has gone wrong, and one hears the flippantly flat little voice of the reviewer (perhaps even of the female sex). With warm affection the poet recalls the rooms of the family house where it (his childhood) was spent. He has been able to imbue with much lyricism the poetic descriptions of objects among which it was spent. When you listen closely . . . We all, attentively and piously ['cautiously' in *Dar*] . . . The strains of the past . . . (22/27)

Fyodor's special emotional ties to his past are debased by the reviewer's clichés, but his poetry does in effect what the reviewer suggests. His language succeeds even as hers fails. Nabokov added to the English translation a number of phrases like 'to coin a phrase' (31), 'to use a Victorian cliché' (34), to draw attention to the parody of conventional formulae in his own texts, and parts of subsequent chapters are parodic tributes to Nabokov's Russian masters.

The chapter continues to develop by modified aposiopesis. Just as the unwritten review occasions a better one, so too does a story which Fyodor rejects as material for the novel he plans to write one day actually constitute part of his literary coming of age. A doomed love triangle and a botched suicide pact involving two young *émigrés* and a Berliner, having been dismissed as 'a banal triangle of tragedy' and 'a suspiciously neat structure' (51/54–55), supplies the young author with the plot of his first attempt at a short story, which is duly included. The plot is as negligible as its dismissive description suggests, but it neatly illustrates Nabokov's particular sort of black humour when dealing with potentially grisly subjects, that lightness, even facetiousness that gives the whole episode an absurdly comic quality *and* its strange poignancy. (Many of Nabokov's short stories work with similar intonations and similarly casual eruptions of violence.)

Nabokov systematically resorts to this tone in order to offer an alternative to the portentous representation of such events. Fyodor writes:

> Any corny man of ideas, any 'serious' novelist in horn-rimmed glasses – the family doctor of Europe and the seismographer of its social tremors – would no doubt have found in this story something highly characteristic of the 'frame of mind of young people in the postwar years' – a combination of words which in itself (even apart from the 'general idea' it conveyed) made me speechless with scorn. (48/52)

The details and incidents of individual existence count for so much in the Nabokovian scheme of things that it is impossible to take seriously the proposition that anything as nebulous as the *Zeitgeist* could have any effect whatever on a real person's behaviour. Anyone coarse or simple-minded enough to be influenced by a collection of dreary clichés is simply not worth bothering about, except as the occasional object of satire. Notice how posing the question in this way deflects attention from the large problem that did affect more than would-be suicides who took newspaper headlines too seriously. The succession of catastrophic events that shook Europe between 1914 and 1938 (the year he finished writing *The Gift*) gave souls as hardy as Nabokov's a sense that Western culture was indeed undergoing a kind of crisis. Of course, those events produced living conditions that became intolerable for people who, lacking his extraordinary resilience and talent, could not deal with their circumstances as successfully as he did. To the extent that it recognizes the plight of such people at all, Nabokov's novel simply refuses to take them seriously. And one need hardly point out that, by the mid-1930s, the list of spiritual crises suffered by Russian writers for whom, understandably, the century seemed relentlessly oppressive, was a very long one indeed.

Fyodor goes to a literary evening where a mediocre play full of 'general ideas' is read out. He and Koncheyev, one of the emigration's most important poets, leave together, and their conversation features a brisk tour of Russian literature during which they exchange various value judgements. Fyodor is harshly dismissive, Koncheyev more temperate, but their colloquy is finally revealed to be as imaginary as the review of Fyodor's poems, merely an exchange that Fyodor would have liked to have with this aloof, admired figure. The effect on the reader is somewhat disorienting. Who is responsible then for all those opinions? Is Dostoevsky really to be regarded as 'Bedlam turned back into Bethlehem' (83/84)? Or Leskov, one of Russian literature's most inventive prose stylists since Gogol and a fascinating example of the multifaceted nature of Russian realism, to be dismissed for his anglicisms? Revealingly, the novel never makes any attempt to elaborate on these judgements, and it is fitting that a text in which the emphasis consistently falls on private love, private passion should have for its heroine a private literature in which the provocative claims of an idiosyncratic iconoclasm count for everything.

In Chapter Two Nabokov attempts the same balancing act that he succeeded with in Chapter One: its ostensible subject is a biography that never gets written; its real subject is what Fyodor learns from his failure to write a biography of his father, a famous lepidopterist who has died in mysterious circumstances during his last expedition. Which makes this chapter, at least in part, that 'unwritten' biography, interspersed with bits of auto-commentary and events in Fyodor's life. The crucial questions raised here are: 'What kind of information does one require to write a biography?' and, 'How does one become a full-fledged writer?' The answer to both is, apparently: 'Read Pushkin for inspiration', and this makes him the tutelary spirit who presides over this chapter as well. Naturally enough, Fyodor's interest in writing a travel narrative that will re-create his father's exploits as a distinguished naturalist makes him seize on a text like *Journey to Arzrum*, Pushkin's account of an 1829 visit to the Caucasus, to serve as a model. The choice is intriguing, because it presents the reader with a number of apparent similarities that mask essential differences, and in the process reveals a great deal about the contrasting arts of Pushkin and Nabokov.

Both works feature an outsider encountering exotic lands and customs, using his particular point of view to emphasize the strangeness of what he sees. Pushkin plays many roles: amateur ethnographer, man of the world, Russian chauvinist, lonely traveller, and so on. But since he is giving us an account of his own travels, even while he projects a number of different personae, he includes the context and circumstances that encouraged or frustrated or affected him during his journey, and this sometimes makes for an engaging sort of self-mockery or self-deprecation. Fyodor is writing an account of someone else's travels, and indulging in a great deal of speculation while he does it. This makes his account the projection of a fantasy, the fantasy of the wise, knowing, fearless, haughty adventurer who scorns most of those he encounters. Fyodor wants to believe this about his father because it will help him justify his own preoccupation with self, but as the biography slips into romantic cliché, he finally abandons it, just as Pushkin abandoned his experiments when they did not work out.

A simple example will help illustrate the contrast. Take the following passage from Pushkin's journey, in which he gives a brief description of a visit to a camp filled with plague victims:

> I didn't dismount and was careful to stay down wind. One of the sick men was taken out of the tent for our inspection; he was extremely pale and staggered as if drunk. Another patient was lying unconscious. Having inspected the plague-stricken man and wished the hapless fellow a quick recovery, I turned my attention to the two Turks who had led him out of the tent, undressed him, touched him, as if the plague was nothing more than a mere cold. I must confess I felt ashamed of my European

timidity in the presence of such indifference, and made haste to
return to the town.[10]

This is Pushkin the reflective, omnivorous observer, taking in every
aspect of the scene, including his own pusillanimity, and conveying
it to us with urbane self-denigration. Here by way of contrast is
Fyodor from Chapter Two of *The Gift* describing his father in similar
circumstances:

> I liked – I only now understood how much I liked it – that special
> easy knack he showed in dealing with a horse, a dog, a gun, a
> bird or a peasant boy with a two-inch splinter in his back – he was
> constantly being brought people who were wounded, maimed,
> even infirm, even pregnant women, who probably took his mys-
> terious occupation for voodoo practice. I liked the fact that, in
> contradistinction to the majority of non-Russian travelers, Sven
> Hedin for example, he never changed his clothes for Chinese
> ones on his wanderings; in general he kept aloof, was severe and
> resolute in the extreme in his relations with the natives, showing
> no indulgence to mandarins and lamas; and in camp he prac-
> tised shooting, which served as an excellent precaution against
> any importuning. . . . And once at an international banquet in
> London (and this episode pleases me most of all), Sven Hedin,
> sitting next to my father, asked him how it had happened that,
> travelling with unprecedented freedom over the forbidden parts
> of Tibet, in the immediate vicinity of Lhasa, he had not gone to
> look at it, to which my father replied that he had not wanted to
> sacrifice even one hour's collecting for the sake of visiting 'one
> more filthy little town' – and I can see so clearly how his eyes
> must have narrowed as he spoke. (128–29/125)

Pushkin is timid and afraid for himself in the presence of the
sick; Fyodor's father has a reputation for healing them. Pushkin
is intrigued by the characteristics of the people he meets that make
them different from him as persons; the butterfly collector remains
an outsider. Pushkin's acquisition of an ethnographer's knowledge
is simply a function of his personality, his fascination with other
sorts of humanity; Nabokov has his hero's father announce a
purist's stance as a defence against the contamination of any kind of
socially useful learning. Pushkin is keen to give his readers a sense
of life as a continuum in which peoples' attitudes change, since just

prior to the visit he describes how he has repulsed a plague victim in the street; Fyodor's father is seen in a variety of contexts but he is always essentially the same. Pushkin's account works primarily at putting the reader in his place; Fyodor's works at one remove, using second-hand material to help him imagine what it must have been like, and thus interposing between the text and the reader his response to the various attitudes struck by his famous father between the text and the reader.

At the end of Chapter Two we learn that Fyodor's most recent change of lodgings will take him 'from Pushkin Avenue to Gogol Street' (164/157), another reference that needs a gloss of some kind if the reader is to plot correctly the implications of this particular move. The visit to Pushkin Avenue has been a necessary stop, but although it has proved inspiring in general terms – Fyodor has learned from Pushkin in the same way that, say, all English dramatists can learn from Shakespeare – he will have to take up residence somewhere else if he is to find his real home.

Nabokov himself wrote a book on Gogol in which he gives a brilliant, deliberately provocative account of what constitutes the essential genius of this strange Russian writer. In his book Nabokov was reacting against those critics who had praised Gogol as the first Russian realist, and then gone on to use him for polemical purposes in the extra-literary battles that have so often characterized Russian criticism. By mocking the sociological critics and instead praising Gogol's lyrical genius, his stylistic innovations, his angularity, and the purity of his nightmarish visions, Nabokov joined the Russian formalists and others who sought to save this genius from the hands of the social reformers.

At first glance, what Nabokov admired in Gogol bears little resemblance to Chapter Three of *The Gift*. In it, we hear about Fyodor's theories of versification and then are treated to some actual samples of his verse disguised as prose. Again the question arises: is this poetry deliberately bad, the product of an aborted visit from an absent-minded muse, or must Fyodor progress as lyric poet as well as novelist? 'To fiction be as to your country true'? 'In honor of your lips when they kiss mine I might devise a metaphor some time'? 'Those are not clouds – but star-high mountain spurs; not lamplit blinds – but camplight on a tent! O swear to me that while the heartblood stirs, you will be true to what we shall invent'? (198/169) Those troubled by the clangy rhymes and the clichéic, Romantic metaphors will find little solace in the Russian originals.

The first is as flat and laconic in *Dar*, the second as corny, and the end of the third in literal translation reads 'O swear that to the end of the road you will be true only to invention'. In other words, even Nabokov's genius as a translator cannot save these lines.

The unadulterated badness of the verse would seem to suggest that Fyodor's gift is not yet fully realized. Zina Mertz, Fyodor's chief admirer and the girl whom fate has apparently arranged for him, evidently takes her name from Mnemo*zina*, the Russian word for the muse of poetry. As only half a muse, i.e. as only the desired figure in an unconsummated relationship, she cannot be responsible for his inspiration at this stage. She has not even made an appearance in the novel yet, because she is more catalyst than heroine, the means by which Fyodor surveys the literature her namesake inspired and he hopes to add to. Like Ganin and Martin, Fyodor is simultaneously attracted and repulsed by the crudity of fleshly desires, and he enjoys his most satisfactory relationship with a woman who represents something of primarily symbolic value to him, his independence. His communing with a muse figure and rejecting the temptations of her simulacra in real life Berlin show how his ideas about desire count for more than actual feelings, how the pursuit of the unattainable can become more prized than its possession.

Women are equally shadowy figures in most of Gogol's fiction, and there are other links as well. Both writers share a fascination with the dreams and nightmares of everyday existence, with its tendency to metamorphose and evanesce, and use a language rich in inventive metaphors to capture these qualities; a conviction that only a extraordinary artist could notice the ordinary; the notion of narrative as a performance that creates its own vitality; an interest in the satiric use of types for comic purposes (the descriptions in *The Gift* of the German natives), the verbal humour and the humour of situation (the farcical meetings at the writer's union).

Yet Nabokov once said in an interview that Gogol was inimitable and that he had learned nothing from him.[11] For one thing, Gogol worked out his own hypochondria, his general obsession with his physical state in complex ways in his novels. For another, he spent an entire career plunging from one work to another in an attempt to please all those critics who were expecting such great things from him and to create himself as a great author. Nabokov did neither. Their attitudes to the world that supplies them with their material are different as well. Here is a typical pronouncement by Gogol about how he sees his role as a writer:

> Fellow countrymen! I too have Russian blood in my veins, like you. Look, I am crying! As a comic actor, before I made you laugh, now I am crying. Allow me to feel that my profession too is just as honourable as that of each of you, that I am serving my land just as all of you are serving, that I am not some frivolous buffoon, created for the amusement of frivolous people, but an honourable civil servant of God's great state.[12]

There is potential irony in such a passage, of course, especially when one thinks of all the time Gogol spent satirizing the honourable civil servants he lauds here, and all the time he spent outside Russia so that he could yearn for his homeland. Nabokov always seems superior to, even supercilious with, most of his characters in a way that Gogol does not. Gogol's characters were his fellow travellers; Nabokov's were 'galley slaves',[13] who under duress took him wherever he wanted to go. This is more than just a question of temperament or artistic proclivity. In *The Gift*, Fyodor knows he will be a great writer because he is an outsider. Those whom he sees on the streets are sometimes described as 'hags' and 'hucksters' because they suspect him to be in possession of a gift which they would like to steal from him. If he allows himself to be vulnerable, they will pounce, so he must simply use them as material for his art, scorning all the while any aesthetic theory that would make him subservient to them by requiring him to serve them.

The combination of models Fyodor imitates provides him with an eclectic, freewheeling style which he uses to tackle his next writing project, the biography of the nineteenth-century radical critic, Nikolay Chernyshevsky, that comprises Chapter Four. This style is ideal for the young writer, as it enables him to be irreverent about one of the saints of progressive thought in Russia, thus developing his comic and satiric gifts, while at the same time he can attempt, in giving the reader more than the official view, to represent him as a complete human being, to see him from the inside as it were. The great advantage of this is that the plaster saint of Soviet hagiography becomes all too human. The disadvantage is that by concentrating so exclusively on the weaknesses of someone like Chernyshevsky, Nabokov sometimes seems to be dismissing the entire radical movement in nineteenth-century Russia as silly. Of course Chernyshevsky, Dobrolyubov, Pisarev *et al.* had as many human problems as any group of dogmatic, intensely committed individuals trying to change a whole society, and Nabokov performs a useful service by reminding us of this and delighting us with his account of their foibles. But after the laughter has died away, and we are left to ponder the significance of what we have read about the epoch and its individuals, the argument in this chapter amounts to the claim that because such critics were so maladroit in managing their human affairs or so doctrinaire in their views on aesthetic matters, their social and political ideas were necessarily flawed. Because literature was the social conscience of nineteenth century Russia, the medium in which ideas about social change were expressed, these critics perforce involved themselves in aesthetic questions. Nabokov claims in *Lectures on Literature* that 'the study of the sociological or political impact of literature has to be devised mainly for those who are by temperament or education immune to the aesthetic vibrancy of authentic literature', but he gives no convincing reasons for the assumption that those interested in sociology or politics are immune to 'aesthetic vibrancy', nor does he convincingly argue for the notion that the only 'authentic literature' is the kind he happens to like.[14] True, the radical critics had the misfortune of being hailed as precursors by those who, once they gained power, systematically silenced and destroyed everyone who disagreed with them, but even Marxism was once on the side of human freedom, and the novel obscures the important differences between the two generations of revolutionaries.

Nabokov attempts to forestall just such objections with the reviews of Fyodor's biography which he includes at the beginning of Chapter Five. Having deplored Fyodor's 'debunking' of the men of the 1860s, one Christopher Mortus (Nabokov's parody of the *émigré* critic Adamovich), insists that 'We, their [the radical critics'] refined and weary grandchildren, also want something that is above all human; we demand the values which are essential to the soul. This "utilitarianism" is more elevated, perhaps, than theirs, but in some respects it is more urgent even than the one they preached'(340/316). Nabokov's objections to such sentiments are bound up with his contempt for their counterparts in his own era, the pro-Soviet, 'progressive' line that a whole generation of critics actually believed and prosletysed for unceasingly between the revolution and the mid-1950s. Though he too is a champion of 'values essential to the soul', he believes no literary group can convey such values. Another critic insists that Fyodor has misunderstood the whole concept of 'epoch', and accuses him of turning history 'into an arbitrary gyration of multicolored spots, into some kind of impressionistic picture' (342/318). For Nabokov, such a view of history is not only aesthetically pleasing but empirically sound, and he expects the reader to see the irony here as being at the expense of the pompous critic.

But the moral outrage in the negative reviews becomes a trifle repetitive after a while, for Nabokov pulls his punches a little. A genuinely challenging critique of Fyodor's book would have asked questions like: 'Is there a point at which the trade-off between satiric success and mimetic accuracy becomes too great?' 'Does Fyodor actually handicap his own attempt to humanize Chernyshevsky by reducing him to a collection of comic "themes"?' Nabokov's hero misrepresents Chernyshevsky's youthful correspondence, ignores diary evidence that invites a more sympathetic reading of his problems with women, caricatures his relationship with his son, oversimplifies the radical critics' attitude to poetry, glosses over Chernyshevsky's considerable gifts as a literary critic, misreads his attitude to Pushkin's work, gives an inaccurate and misleading account of his views on specialized studies, and tendentiously summarizes the debate that swirled around literature and politics in the 1850s and 1860s.[15] By refusing to print Chapter Four in the 1939 version of *The Gift* that was published, the editors of *Sovremennye Zapiski* (*Contemporary Annals*) inadvertently confirmed the novel's point about the intolerance of those who insist on a social component for literature, and at the same time pre-empted a debate that might have helped make clear the complexities of the issues involved. The critical comments by Koncheyev, in a second imaginary dialogue between him and Fyodor, come much closer to the mark, particularly when Fyodor imagines him mentioning reworking of sources, but Koncheyev contends that this is stylistic reworking only. He also notes that Fyodor's grasp of parody is uncertain, that parody can become seriousness, which can in turn become a mannerism, but the general impact of such accurate critical claims is lessened by characterizing them as trivial.

As far as Fyodor's literary progress is concerned, the satiric portrait of Chernyshevsky does provide him with an outlet for the aggressive tendencies that he must transform into creative energy. The biography also enables him to vent a number of literary critical opinions that demonstrate his maturity as an assessor of literature.

Best known in the West as the era of the great development of the realistic novel, nineteenth-century Russian literature as construed by Nabokov is a rather lean affair, since he would exclude Dostoevsky, Goncharov, Leskov and Saltykov-Shchedrin, not to mention all the minor novelists like Druzhinin and Pisemsky, from any list of figures that should be considered important for literary reasons. This makes him an advocate of art for art's sake, but not quite in the sense that Oscar Wilde or one of the French decadents would have used the phrase. For them, their aesthetic was bound up with a moral pose, a desire to '*épater le bourgeois*' by flouting his moral code and flaunting their own. Nabokov has no moral dispute with the bourgeois; quite the contrary, in novel after novel he will endorse positions on sexual mores, individual responsibility, social and political questions that are virtually indistinguishable from those taken by the defenders of middle-class morality. No, what he has in common with the position defined by Wilde is a contempt for the aggressive philistinism of that class, for its assuming to dictate aesthetic criteria to lonely geniuses, for its ignorant worship of the third rate, for its hopeless infatuation with its own shoddy materialistic ideals. The Wilde who said 'The views of illiterates on art are unaccountable'[16] was expressing Nabokov's own views precisely.

The rest of Chapter Five deals with the three main plot lines of the novel: the story of the Chernyshevsky family, the literary activities of the *émigrés* in Berlin, and Fyodor's own relationship with Zina Mertz. The first provides more opportunity for musing about death. When Alexander Chernyshevsky dies, he toys with the idea of an afterlife, only to reject it because 'religion subsumes a suspicious facility of general access that destroys the value of its revelations' (347/322). Yet his conviction that there is no such thing as a world beyond this one, asserted in the very last words he speaks, is immediately undercut. When Fyodor takes up the same speculations can make nothing of this momentous question:

> He was in a troubled and obscured state of mind which was incomprehensible to him, just as everything was incomprehensible, from the sky to that yellow tram rumbling along the clear track of the Hohenzollerndamm . . . but gradually his annoyance with himself passed and with a kind of relief – as if the responsibility for his soul belonged not to him but to someone who knew what it all meant – he felt that all this skein of random

thoughts, like everything else as well – the seams and sleaziness ['shafts of light' in *Dar*] of the spring day, the ruffle of the air, the coarse, variously intercrossing threads of confused sounds – was but the reverse side of a magnificent fabric, on the front of which there gradually formed and became alive images invisible to him. (352/326)

This faith in the ultimate harmony of everything, the personalizing of the conviction by imagining a 'someone' who is 'responsible', the certainty that only by paying meticulous attention to details and their complex interrelations can one make all this, in this life at any rate, any less incomprehensible – these concerns were to occupy Nabokov the whole of his adult life. In a journal written when he was eighteen, he notes: 'Until science resolves the question more soundly, we are still doomed to annihilation. . . . The existence of eternal life is an invention of human cowardice; its denial, a lie to one's self. Whoever says "There is no soul, no immortality" secretly thinks "but maybe?"'[17] And in the fiction written in his last two decades, Nabokov made this an even more explicit subject of his fiction.

The novel comes to no definite conclusion on such a question (how could it?), but in two separate passages Nabokov includes some crucial remarks on this interest in a transcendent realm. The first occurs during yet another 'imaginary experience', this time Fyodor's dream about the return of his dead father. Clearly the whole attempt to reconstitute the past in Nabokov is in one sense an attempt to deal with the loss of his father as a young adult. The appearance of the father does not so much give him a clue about the existence of the after life as it does a clue about this one. Earlier in this connection we read:

In and around my father, around this clear and direct strength, there was something difficult to convey in words, a haze, a mystery, an enigmatic reserve which made itself felt sometimes more, sometimes less. It was as if this genuine, very genuine man possessed an aura of something still unknown but which was perhaps the most genuine of all. It had no direct connection either with us, or with my mother, or with the externals of life . . . it was neither pensiveness nor melancholy . . . I cannot track down a name for his secret, but I only know that that was the source of that special – neither glad nor morose, having indeed no

connection with the outward appearance of human emotions
– solitude to which neither my mother nor all the entomologists
of the world had any admittance. (130–31/126–27)

The language of the passage is striking for a number of reasons.
Firstly, it reminds us of how often when things become very important in Nabokov he points out how inadequate language is, or
interlaces his text with the 'somehow's and the 'perhaps's of
the amateur metaphysician. This forces the argument to proceed
again by aposiopesis, that rhetorical flourish that leaves the author
gesturing at an absence. All the negatives in the passage quoted tell
us what the secret is not, but not what it is. Nabokov implies that
Fyodor's father has such a firm yet relaxed sense of his own selfhood
that he has been given a glimpse of this beyond whose existence
Nabokov suspects. As a ghostly presence, he is there in the dream
to confirm for the boy that his guess was correct; the underside of
the carpet metaphor *does* contain an important truth about human
life. Yet can it be stated more clearly or in more detail?

The recent investigations of this aspect of Nabokov's work prove
conclusively just how important questions about 'the otherworld'
were for him, but Nabokov was always reluctant to make too
definite or solemn such propositions. The emphasis in the novel
is insistently on the strangeness of this world, and that quality of it
makes Fyodor ultimately content to live with the obstacles it poses
to absolute knowledge. Chesterton notes in one essay that he always
found it easy to accept God's conditions for human life because 'it
seemed to me that existence was itself so very eccentric a legacy that
I could not complain of not understanding the limitations of the
vision when I did not understand the vision they limited. The frame
was no stranger than the picture'.[18] The phrasing catches precisely
the tension between the intrigue of mystery and the acceptance
of mortality in Nabokov's novel, and helps explain why he, like
Chesterton, made the 'eccentric legacy' his main subject.

The ending of *The Gift* also hints at this miraculous world which
exists beyond the confines of the earthly text in which we read
about it, and provides Nabokov with an indeterminate yet pro-
foundly satisfying conclusion. Fyodor and Zina are returning to the
house which has with miraculous suddenness become a place where
they can consummate their love in complete privacy. Yet Fyodor's
penchant for misplacing his keys will deny them entry to the house,
and we as readers know this as he nears his goal, while he does not.

So The End is not to be the end, at least not quite. But Nabokov means more by his tentative conclusion than this:

> Good-by, my book! Like mortal eyes, imagined ones must close some day. Onegin from his knees will rise – but his creator strolls away. And yet the ear cannot right now part with the music and allow the tale to fade; the chords of fate itself continue to vibrate; and no obstruction for the sage exists where I have put The End: the shadows of my world extend beyond the skyline of the page, blue as tomorrow's morning haze – nor does this terminate the phrase.[19] (411/378)

This says that those who are attuned to my methods by now will realize that the end is never the end, that just as my hero's father was resurrected, so too can my characters continue to exist in the realm created by the joint imaginative effort of author and reader. And not only that: the underside of the magnificent design that life sometimes seems to hint at is an analogy for one's response to a work of literary art, one's sense of the unity in diversity that constitutes any major work, including that of the 'other V.N., Visible Nature'.[20] All the references to dawn and haze and 'shadows of my world' invoke that luminescent, vaguely surreal world of border and transition states that signals the indeterminate nature of certain limits thought by the unimaginative to be finite.

The reference to *Eugene Onegin*, Russian literature's most famous 'novel in verse', helps illustrate both points. At the end of that poem, Onegin is on his knees to the girl he once spurned, and, according to Nabokov at any rate, he has every reason to hope that her refusal is not as final as many commentators would like us to believe. By seeing in her answer 'a confession of love that must have made Eugene's experienced heart leap with joy', by contrasting the rhetorical forcefulness of her 'anguished, poignant, palpitating, enchanting, almost voluptuous, almost alluring enjambments' with '[t]he hollow perfunctory sound of the pat couplet'[21] with which she rejects Onegin, Nabokov indicates that the impact of Pushkin's emotional art should be clear to those readers who want the two lovers to consummate their love, who are yearning for a closure that will be a new beginning. The endings of Pushkin's poem and Nabokov's novel, then, bring together a matrix of harmonies: the reader's response to the implications of the closed yet open text makes it live on, guarantees the author literary immortality, and hints at the personal immortality that awaits those who refuse to countenance, in life or in art, the idea of an ending.

In the next chapter, we shall consider some of the Russian novels in which Nabokov explores a different sort of consciousness. In these novels he asks himself, 'How would life look if I gave some of the interest in the way life reveals its patterns to characters who are limited or narrow or obsessed or mad?' An exuberant black humour, an impressive technical mastery, and a distinctively Nabokovian view of the world are the result.

3

Studies in Obsession: *The Defense, The Eye, Laughter in the Dark,* and *Despair*

This chapter is devoted to four of Nabokov's Russian novels, *The Defense, The Eye, Laughter in the Dark,* and *Despair*. They were all published in the 1930s, and I propose to discuss them as studies of obsession. This schematic way of proceeding has the advantage of isolating what eventually came to be *the* central feature of Nabokovian narrative: the plot that organizes itself around one all-consuming idea of the central character. The limitation of this sort of criticism is that at times it can require its practitioners to do so much hacking away at ill-fitting details that they make Procrustes look like a masseur, but I have tried to avoid that in what follows by discussing some of the features that differentiate the novels as well.

Another potential problem with this approach is that Nabokov always insisted his characters' *idées fixes* were just a stylistic device, the means by which the plot unfolded, and therefore did not easily lend themselves to any kind of psychological reading. In the Foreword to *The Defense*, for example, he includes a warning for what he calls 'the Viennese delegation':

> Analysts and analyzed will enjoy, I hope, certain details of the treatment Luzhin is subjected to after his breakdown (such as the curative insinuation that a chess player sees Mom in his

Queen and Pop in his opponent's King), and the little Freudian who mistakes a Pixlok set for the key to a novel will no doubt continue to identify my characters with his comic-book notion of my parents, sweethearts and serial selves.

The crudity of some aspects of Freudian psychology lends itself admirably to this kind of humour, but as a rebuttal of Freud this says in effect: because when I write I am conscious of the possibility of others attributing subconscious motives to my characters or to me, as revealed in my choice of situation and symbol, I have anticipated this reading by including my own mockery of it; therefore, the interest of my novels lies elsewhere.

Critics have tended to take him at his word, yet in each of the novels under consideration here, the psychological motivation, the 'sweethearts' and the 'serial selves' of the characters are of considerable interest. My purpose in this chapter is to talk about the way Nabokov deals with obsessions, with a view to including whatever evidence, clinical or otherwise, that seems germane to a discussion of them. When Freud writes about patients using a kind of 'negative magic' to evade the consequences of an experience and convince themselves that the experience itself never happened, or insists we all have 'case histories' in the sense that all our lives represent the working out of elaborate fantasies, or points out that 'wherever natural barriers in the way of satisfaction have not sufficed, mankind has created conventional ones to enjoy love', or remarks that 'A man who doubts his own love may or rather *must* doubt every lesser thing',[1] he supplies a language that helps us to understand the situations that Nabokov isolates and dramatizes in these novels. To exclude such material from consideration, merely because Nabokov makes fun of Freud's ideas which are most easily caricatured, is to impose unnecessary limitations at the outset.

The Defense is about a man obsessed with chess and chess patterns, and Nabokov gives us his life in stages. No doubt one of the things that so impressed *émigré* critics when *The Defense* first appeared was its superbly realized account of the hero as a precocious child. (The Russian novel, unlike its English and French counterparts, does not often enter the world of the child.) Consider the following passage, in which Luzhin recalls his childhood illnesses:

> he remembered especially the time when he was quite small, playing all alone, and wrapping himself up in the tiger rug,

to represent, rather forlornly, a king – it was nicest of all to represent a king since the imaginary mantle protected him against the chills of fever, and he wanted to postpone for as long as possible that inevitable moment when they would feel his forehead, take his temperature and then bundle him into bed. Actually, there had been nothing quite comparable to his October chess-permeated illness. The gray-haired Jew who used to beat Chigorin, the corpse of his aunt's admirer muffled in flowers, the sly, gay countenance of his father bringing a magazine, and the geography teacher petrified with the suddenness of the mate, and the tobacco-smoke-filled room at the chess club where he was closely surrounded by a crowd of university students, and the clean-shaven face of the musician holding for some reason the telephone receiver like a violin, between shoulder and cheek – all this participated in his delirium and took on the semblance of a kind of monstrous game on a spectral, wobbly, and endlessly disintegrating board. (78/55)

The exquisite rendering of the loneliness of a child, the maniacal acuity with which he recalls various scenes, the eerie combination of blur and specificity peculiar to delirium, the way an obsession assumes a metaphoric shape that ultimately transforms one's world – all these details help to characterize young Luzhin. They also recall some of those sections of Nabokov's autobiography in which he remembers his own childhood. There Nabokov suggests that this sort of fever-induced meditation can occasion a 'mind dilation effect';[2] in *The Defense* this effect ultimately becomes the madness which Luzhin can only escape by committing suicide. The passage also vividly recreates the way a child's world is haunted by the faces of the people who inhabit it, the mystery of personality written there in a hand that he yearns to decipher. In more general terms, this description also reminds us just how traditional a novelist Nabokov was at the outset of his career. The autonomy of the individual self and its presentation as character, the existence of shared system of ethical norms, the general emphasis on unity and coherence of plot with its cause-and-effect development – all these are calculated to create in the reader the calm certainty invited by the nineteenth-century novels which so much of *The Defense* imitates, with considerable success. As order and meaning disappear in the nightmare world that overtakes Luzhin, they manifest themselves in the solidity of the frame which sets them off.

In the other early novels organized around an obsession, Nabokov manages to involve his readers by using the twisted view of the world such complexes produce to characterize everyone and every thing the protagonist encounters. Neurosis leads to a hypersensitivity that casts a bizarre light on the ordinary and lends every scene a particular strangeness. This works well for the objects that occupy Luzhin's world, but because the hero is so insensitive to the people around him so much of the time (his personality sometimes borders on the clichéic, the solemn, introspective loner who comes alive only at the chess board), the omniscient narrator must make up for his character's obliviousness by adding lengthy discursive passages.

Consider Luzhin's wife, for example. Nabokov's male heroes are generally either cruelly tortured or lovingly tended by the women who attract them. Luzhin belongs to the second category, and a great deal of the middle section of the novel is taken up with his chess exploits and the transplanted Russia this woman, her family, and their acquaintances have created in Germany. When Luzhin finally understands that he has fallen in love with her, Nabokov simply appends a long list of her traits and then informs us: 'nobody yet had been able to dig down to what was most captivating about her: this was the mysterious ability of her soul to apprehend in life only that which had once attracted and tormented her in childhood, the time when the soul's instinct is infallible' (115/83). This 'infallible instinct' turns out to be the fact that she cares deeply about animals in pain. Thus Luzhin's wife is one of those characters who serve as indices of moral uprightness, and who exist in Nabokov's fiction in order to smooth the way for genius, which they admire but do not understand. Often a trifle stodgy and dull, they none the less embody an ethical standard by which all the other normal (that is, untalented) characters can be judged. She is even permitted to articulate Nabokov's views on the whole question of the emigration and the state of the Soviet Union: 'both here and in Russia people tortured, or desired to torture, other people, but there the torture and desire to torture were a hundred times greater than here and therefore here was better' (237/178). The Dickens who believed that the world would be a better place if people were nicer to each other had a great deal in common with his twentieth-century admirer.

Obsessed with finding a defence that will make him invulnerable to a particularly powerful and innovative opponent, he has a breakdown. The rest of the novel features his wife's ultimately futile attempts to protect his fragile emotional state, and the casual, unexpected ways in which the game reasserts its presence in his life. In the end Luzhin, suffering paranoid delusions that turn the whole world into a board on which an implacable adversary plays his cunning moves, commits suicide by jumping from a window into a chasm which 'was seen to divide into dark and pale squares'(267/201), the chess game he cannot escape. The inevitability of the ending leaves us searching for some sort of allegorical solace. Perhaps Stuart Hampshire is right:

> the voice of the idealistic daughter cannot penetrate the hero's defence, and cannot restore him to some sight of reality, just because hers is the only voice of Russian idealism, of that peculiar native compassion, represented in Gogol and Dostoevsky, which loves absurdity and weakness and looks for the opportunity of self-sacrifice in their defence. The man who loves form and intellectual order is always a stranger to her. Since the marriage between compassion and a sense of order cannot be consummated, the Russian genius must destroy himself. The separation of Christian feeling from the entirely abstract, mathematical intellect – the two aspects of Russian genius – is final. Nothing is left.[3]

Or perhaps we should take comfort in way 'compassion and a sense of order' come together in the sensibility of the novelist himself.

The chess patterns have a curious place in the overall design. Nabokov says in the Foreword: 'Rereading this novel today, replaying the moves of its plot, I feel rather like Anderssen fondly recalling his sacrifice of both Rooks to the unfortunate and noble Kieseritsky – who is doomed to accept it over and over again through an infinity of textbooks, with a question mark for monument.' The analogy between author and chess player at first seems inexact: Against whom does he play? His 'doomed' protagonist? The realistic novel whose conventions he exploits and extends? The reader? But poor Luzhin cannot play on the same board as his creator since he inhabits a different order of reality. The novel and its practitioners are equally implausible as opponents for Nabokov's supremely confident game, and if the reader is someone to be defeated, then the author begins with such an advantage that whatever victory he wins must be a rather hollow one.

The point is made clearer if one knows something of the actual chess game alluded to here. As D. Barton Johnson has shown,[4] the reference is to the 'Immortal Game' played in 1851 that contained perhaps the most brilliant combination ever played, a series of moves that cost Anderssen his queen, both rooks and a bishop but led to an inevitable mate. Johnson notes that the point of giving up one's rooks is to isolate the opponent's king's strongest defender, his queen; he also points out that Kieseritsky was the victim of the double rook sacrifice not once but twice in his career, and that Luzhin's wife is twice separated from him at crucial moments, leading to his insanity and suicide. This explains the cryptic significance of Nabokov's allusion, but there is a more general point about the game between author and reader to be made as well. Kieseritsky must have realized a number of moves before the end that mate was inevitable, yet he chivalrously accepted his doom. Anderssen's combination required a co-operative opponent, someone 'noble' enough, to use Nabokov's word, not to resign, to allow the mating net to be woven in all its glorious complexity. Like Nabokov's novel, chess played at the grandmaster level involves technical mastery, depth of vision, an aesthetic sense, and unerring intuition. The beauties of both are ultimately the product of a co-operative enterprise. Kieseritsky greatly admired the brilliance of his genial opponent, and Anderssen a few years later would laugh with genuine pleasure as he reset the pieces after being demolished by the stunningly innovative chess of the brilliant young American, Paul Morphy. If the reader is as attentive to the details as the author wants, he or she will also be the co-creator of a masterpiece. He 'wins' in the same way that Anderssen did: he succeeds in realizing his vision, but even when temporarily fooled or floundering, he has assisted as the 'idea' of the game was distilled and worked out.

The Defense does represent a real advance in Nabokov's development as a novelist, one that involves the elaborate structure in which Luzhin's life and death are encapsulated, the verbal echoes, 'wayside murmurs' of hidden themes that came to be a Nabokov signature. Such patterning has been the subject of a great deal of stimulating commentary, and one critic has argued quite plausibly that an extremely subtle matrix of clues hints that Luzhin's dead grandfather, a musician, has manœuvred events so that Luzhin becomes a chess player, and thus has enjoyed vicariously the harmonies that his grandson finds on the chess-board.[5] Having compared Nabokov to Bach and Shakespeare, he summarizes *The Defense* this way:

> He considers memory and our relation to our past, fate and our relation to our future, and the intolerant advance of human time. He charts the strange position of human consciousness and explores the possibility that a hereafter may hold some richer relation to time and the self. He wonders whether the independent particulars of our world may form some design we cannot see, and whether our random life may conceal some almost unimaginable artfulness beyond.[6]

Armed with such a description, readers might well be surprised to find that not one of the above topics is tackled discursively in the actual text of *The Defense*. For Nabokov, an interest in consciousness or time or the complicated process of self-creation precludes discursive treatment, for that would mean arguing with the words of the world, the way Thomas Mann or Jean-Paul Sartre would do. The mere presence of the hidden patterns must serve in lieu of any kind of metaphysical argument, and Nabokov is such a careful craftsman that his work always affords another pattern for his more diligent readers. For the sceptical, it will not be exactly clear what wondering about the hereafter by hinting at its patterns can provide except one more pattern. Invited to posit links between motifs in a novel and 'the independent particulars of some world we cannot see', they will wonder why they should. So too with estimations of value. Those who place a priority on complexity and who are willing to endorse the 'well-made artefact' aesthetic which it encourages will have no great difficulty in seeing the merits of this novel; those with different criteria can simply demur. *The Defense* announced the advent of a important new talent, but it will be an early 'masterpiece' only for those primarily interested in matters architectonic.

The next in the sequence of 'obsession' novels is *The Eye*, to all appearances a much slighter work. Nabokov wrote it in a few months soon after completing *The Defense* (it was published serially in 1930, but not in book form until 1938), and it is really more a novella than a novel. In one important respect though it marks a major departure for him, and represents the first of the novels in a clear line that runs through *Despair* to *Lolita* and *Pale Fire*. The main achievement of these novels is the creation of a certain kind of voice: hypnotic, eloquent, humorous, alternately lyrical and prosaic, elated and depressed, earnestly importunate, hopelessly egocentric, eager to convince, yet dubious about the ability of mere words ever to convince. *The Eye* features an early, undeveloped version of this voice, but its basic traits are unmistakable.

In all these novels the voice is forced to speak by a profound emotional crisis, one which leads to the violent death of the people involved in it. The attempt to create a story which articulates the meaning of the crisis and its consequences makes the experience of the narrator cognate with those of the reader he so insistently imagines, because both are engaged in sorting through alternative plot sequences, finding patterns, and attributing significance to what has happened. In *The Eye* the crisis in question is the narrator's suicide attempt, prompted by his physical humiliation at the hands of a jealous husband he has cuckolded, but there is much in the text to indicate that even before this occurs he is emotionally unstable. From the outset he looks askance on his own puny pleasures and characterizes himself as an extreme version of one of Nabokov's dualists, always watching himself, always detached.

In the Foreword Nabokov claims to have made Smurov a Russian *émigré* simply because he happened to like Russian expatriates in his 'literary youth', adding that the characters in the novel 'might just as well have been Norwegians in Naples or Ambracians in Ambridge' because he has 'always been indifferent to social problems'. Yet his *émigré* is clearly a version of the loveless, spectral people that Gogol and Dostoevsky depicted (the St Petersburg that many of their heroes hail from is mentioned on page one of Nabokov's novel), and his loss of country and therefore identity in one cataclysmic event has made a weak and unbalanced nature more vulnerable. The chief difference between Nabokov and his great predecessors is not the way he floats free from any political context, but rather his willingness to ground the events of his narrative in the real by consistently providing a series of naturalistic explanations for everything that happens. He presents the novel as a sort of puzzle in his Introduction, but unlike Gogol and Dostoevsky, Nabokov has everywhere provided hints that lead to its 'solution'. (Nabokov notes in the Foreword: 'It is unlikely that even the most credulous peruser of this twinkling tale will take long to realize who Smurov is. I tried it on an old English lady, two graduate students, an ice-hockey coach, a doctor, and the twelve-year-old child of a neighbor. The child was the quickest, the neighbor, the slowest'.)

Here is a passage from an early scene in which the narrator attempts to commit suicide and fails comically:

> Some time later, if one can speak here of time at all, it became clear that after death human thought lives on by momentum. I was tightly swaddled in something – was it a shroud? was it simply taut darkness? I remembered everything – my name, life on earth – with perfect clarity, and found wonderful comfort in the thought that now there was nothing to worry about. With mischievous and carefree logic I progressed from the incomprehensible sensation of tight bandages to the idea of a hospital, and, at once obedient to my will, a spectral hospital ward materialized around me, and I had neighbors, mummies like me, three on either side. What a mighty thing was human thought, that it could hurtle on beyond death! (19/30–31)

Throughout the novel, Nabokov deftly exploits for comic purposes the ironic gap that yawns between the narrator's self-flattering delusions and his humdrum reality, but there is pathos in such delusions as well. All the talk of clarity and thought and playful logic point to a need to escape emotional problems in this world, rather than discoveries regarding the mysteries of the next. The more plebian explanation of the events described – that the suicide attempt has not succeeded, that the narrator is a failure in death as in life, and that the world is at least as mighty as the human thought that attempts to banish it – haunts the novel from this point on.

The narrator solves his problem (and Nabokov neatly solves the problem of telling the story of a 'non-existent' person) by creating a double, one Smurov, whom he invests with all the *savoir faire* and manly accomplishments that he lacks. The double comes to Russian literature via the Gothic romance, the novels of Mrs Radcliffe and the stories of Hoffmann, and its first appearance is in Gogol's 'The Nose', which influenced Dostoevsky's 'The Double', the next great Russian experiment in the genre. In the first story, a minor official loses his nose, only to find it travelling about town in a carriage, and impudently refusing to go back where it belongs. In the second, the same atmosphere of stultifying bureaucracy and its psychic wounds obtains, this time afflicting a Mr Golyadkin, whose place in the hierarchy of officialdom is taken by his own double. The confrontation between the two Golyadkins clearly represents for Dostoevsky the battle between those burdened with a shaky sense of self and those with no anxieties whatever on that score. Nabokov's protagonist descends in a direct line from these characters. The double he becomes obsessed with appears to be having considerable success in courting a young Russian *émigrée*, nicknamed Vanya, but he is eventually exposed as a braggart and a slanderer in whom Vanya, engaged to be married to someone else, is totally uninterested. At this point the narrator ceases to distinguish between himself and his double, and the story ends when the cuckolded husband seeks him out, lets the reader in on 'the secret' of the narrator's identity by calling him 'Smurov', and makes peace with him. Smurov concludes:

> I do not exist: there exist but the thousands of mirrors that reflect me. With every acquaintance I make, the population of phantoms resembling me increases. Somewhere they live, somewhere they multiply. . . .
>
> And yet I am happy. Yes, happy. I swear, I swear I am happy. I have realized that the only happiness in this world is to observe, to spy, to watch, to scrutinize oneself and others, to be nothing but a big, slightly vitreous, somewhat bloodshot, unblinking eye. I swear that this is happiness. What does it matter that I am a bit cheap, a bit foul, and that no one appreciates all the remarkable things about me – my fantasy, my erudition, my literary gift . . . And what do I care if she marries another? Every other night I dream of her dresses and things on an endless clothesline of bliss, in a ceaseless wind of possession, and her husband shall never learn what I do to the silks and fleece of the dancing witch. This is love's supreme accomplishment. I am happy – yes, happy! What more can I do to prove it, how to proclaim that I am happy? Oh, to shout it so that all of you believe me at last, you cruel, smug people.[7] (86–87/113–14)

The Gogolian offhandedness of the imagery makes the novel suddenly soar just when one is prepared for it to drift quietly away. Here is the exultation of the solipsist without a self to sustain the illusion of his unique existence, as well as the final clue that the strange split disturbing so many of Nabokov's protagonists has sexual frustrations for a basis. This carries over to become a frustration with language itself, even as the words give away more than madman realizes. The reference to 'literary gift' is jarring – the narrator is not an aspiring writer but a humble tutor and drudge – and it is almost as if Nabokov is including here a detáil that will be crucial in novels like *Despair* and *Lolita*, as if he temporarily forgets that he has not explored the links between the schizophrenic eye that paralyzes spontaneity, turning its owner into someone who has nothing to introspect but his own introspection, and 'the eye' as detached observer who re-creates what he sees. Note also Smurov's oddly gratuitous references to his own cheapness and foulness. Here Nabokov gestures at a Dostoevskian self-loathing and the paradoxical pleasures such feelings evoke, but unlike Dostoevsky's famous anti-hero, the Underground Man, Smurov is not vile enough to be loathsome, or shrewd enough to despise himself, but rather a pathetic and forlorn solitary whom life has simply bypassed.

The sympathy Smurov evokes is the sympathy that Nabokov always invites his readers to extend to those vital enough to have an imagination. Just as Gogol's and Dostoevsky's beleaguered souls seem preferable to those who would lock them up in the madhouse, so too is Smurov's preposterous account of his life presented as more real than the ordinary concerns of those around him. Besides, his private obsession harms no one. Nabokov's comic critique of Marxism in *The Eye* is there to remind us that that is not always the case:

> It is silly to seek a basic law, even sillier to find it. Some mean-spirited little man decides that the whole course of humanity can be explained in terms of insidiously revolving signs of the zodiac or as the struggle between an empty and a stuffed belly; he hires a punctilious Philistine to act as Clio's clerk, and begins a wholesale trade in epochs and masses; and then woe to the private individuum, with his two poor u's, hallooing hopelessly amid the dense growth of economic causes. Luckily no such laws exist: a toothache will cost a battle, a drizzle cancel an insurrection. Everything is fluid, everything depends on chance, and all in vain were the efforts of that crabbed bourgeois in Victorian checkered trousers, author of *Das Kapital*, the fruit of insomnia and migraine. (25/37–38)

The lucky accident, or Cleopatra's nose theory of history, has had its proponents, but even its most fervent adherents are unlikely to dismiss mass movements or economic causes quite so sweepingly, or put them on a par with astrological signs. What Nabokov's witty characterization of Marxism does, however, is make clear that as a novelist he will avoid the swampy areas mapped out by political philosophers, and concentrate instead on the eccentric, the individual and the specific. The irrational standards and chaotic imaginings of the Smurovs of the world announce Nabokov's faith in the subjective vision, because, despite all its neuroses, it could never wreak the sort of havoc that Marx's disciples were responsible for, and because it alone can put us in contact with the world of the spirit.

Laughter in the Dark occupies a curious position in the Nabokov canon. It is his best known Russian novel, yet all the things that make it popular with a general audience – crisp narrative line, sharply etched irony, blackest of black humour – have seemed too crude, too obvious, too easy for those most intrigued by the aspects of Nabokov's work which appeal mainly to an academic readership, and as a result the book has been systematically slighted by his critics.[8] True, *Kamera Obskura*, the Russian version of the novel, shows signs of haste, but when one considers that it was, along with *The Defense*, *The Eye*, and *Glory*, his fourth novel in a couple of years, what he does accomplish in it seems rather remarkable. As another novel of obsession, it most compellingly explores the sexual desire that drives Nabokov's heroes; as an artefact, it anticipates some of the complicated games with the novel he was later to play.

In *The Defense*, we saw how an obsession with aesthetic patterns eventually alienates Luzhin from the physical world altogether. Smurov also attempts to replace reality with his creation because his fantasies are so much more appealing than the humdrum world which contemptuously insults and ignores him. In *Laughter in the Dark* Nabokov works a new variation on this theme, for it tells the story of a man, Albert Albinus, who also throws over his boring life to live in a fantasy world, but here the disastrous consequences stem from his actually realizing his desire, not from his frustrated attempts to will it into existence. The old saw about being careful not to wish for something because you might get it is in effect the moral of Albinus's story. A paradigmatic fairy tale simplicity, then, an exploration of the idea that desire can manifest itself as a kind of madness, a study of the connections between sex, art, and violence, and of an obsession that makes the egocentric wreak comic havoc on everything around him – all these concerns of the mature Nabokov are found in embryo here.

The novel begins with a one-paragraph plot summary, followed by a brief authorial comment:

> Once upon a time there lived in Berlin, Germany, a man called Albinus. He was rich, respectable, happy; one day he abandoned his wife for the sake of a youthful mistress; he loved; was not loved; and his life ended in disaster.
>
> This is the whole of the story and we might have left it at that had there not been profit and pleasure in the telling; and although there is plenty of space on a gravestone to contain, bound in moss, the abridged version of a man's life, detail is always welcome. (7) [9]

The passage reminds us that there are any number of ways of telling the story of a person's life. Even to choose to recount that life as a story, with a shape, a sudden change in fortune, and a dramatic conclusion is to begin with something other than a 'neutral' approach to one's material. In other words, the book promises to present us with not just a series of events but with an attitude towards them. The other thing such a summary draws our attention to is what it promises, forcing us to ponder what 'profit and pleasure' there can be in retelling such a story. Here Nabokov hints at the cautionary and the contradictory nature of such tales, since the story of this man's life and its disaster will solicit our ethical attention even as it affords us pleasure by giving us time off from affairs which solicit such attentions.

All the events are conveyed to the reader through the complex workings of black humour, and although both violence and death are presented as genuinely terrifying, both are repeatedly associated with blissful release as well. The equation is made clear at the end of the first chapter during a conversation in which Albinus's mind wanders back to the young usherette who has made him wonder about the attractions of infidelity. He talks of his interest in her as a kind of madness, thinks about telling his wife or seeing a psychoanalyst, and then there is a pause, and his thought is not completed, but merely indicated as an absence made present with an ellipse. The omniscient author continues: 'No, you can't take a pistol and plug a girl you don't even know, simply because she attracts you' (13). By communicating this crucial, and at this point rather surprising, bit of information as a piece of wry authorial commentary, Nabokov underlines the double perspective the novel proposes in identifying male sexuality and violence. On the one hand, Albinus's curious obsession, his jealousy that precedes actual possession, will be the cause of his comic predicament, the cuckolded adulterer, chronicled so lovingly in scene after scene for our amusement. On the other, it represents an example of the latent passion Nabokov is interested in exploring, and its attractiveness – both as a quasi-sexual fantasy for someone like Albinus, and as a vicarious thrill for the reader. When Freud asserts in *Civilization and Its Discontents* that aggressiveness 'forms the basis of every relation of affection and love',[10] he makes a claim that Nabokov would no doubt reject as reductive psychology, but in novel after novel he gives examples of the link Freud posits. (Nabokov is also fascinated by the vulgar allure of adultery, that aspect of it that made a contemporary Italian film-maker once describe it as the last drama left in the life of the bourgeois. When Nabokov had an affair which he hid from his wife he wrote to his mistress about 'the inevitable vulgarity of deceit'.)[11]

The next chapter is a flashback that encapsulates Albinus's love-life, describes his actual visits to the movie theatre, and ends this way: 'Damn it all, I'm happy, what more do I need? That creature gliding about in the dark. . . . Like to crush her beautiful throat. Well, she is dead anyway, since I shan't go there any more' (23). Here the links between sex and violence become that much clearer, and the idea of this woman's 'painful beauty' becomes more than just a vague oxymoron. The scenes in which Albinus first sees her are illuminated by the light of the screen, on which more violent scenes occur, but they, like his violent desire, are incomprehensible. We learn later that the man with a revolver pursuing the girl and driving the car around hairpin turns on a steep hill is Albinus himself, that he is seeing here scenes from the life that will ineluctably unfold for him once he takes up with this girl. Hence the violence is there for our benefit as re-readers, and it reminds us of just how bound up with the Nabokov novel, both its content and form, is the fascination with transgressions generally. By multiplying fictional levels in this way, Nabokov certainly posits the shifting nature of the novel's relation to reality, but he also hints at something that is always mimetic at the level of human desire, and does so in ways that identify the protagonist's desire for fulfilment with the reader's curiosity to know, and then links them both to the violence and death that end Albinus's life and his story.

The plot is an elaborate one by Nabokov standards, but it is easily orchestrated in the sense that all of its twists and turns are caused by the sexual desires of the principal characters. Albinus sets his young mistress up in an apartment, and when his wife finds out about it, he is forced to choose between staid contentment and fiery ecstasy (or so he imagines it). Much is made of Margot's childlike qualities – she has 'girlish hips' (57/84), her body has 'childish lines' (62/92), she is 'a child herself' (122/180) – because Albinus is at first attracted by her (purely notional) 'purity', and because as a childlike woman she can better represent for him the play world, the world beyond adult responsibilities, the secret world of sexual experimentation that he has fantasized about. In this context the phrase 'everything was permissible' (84) emphasizes the link with those situations that Dostoevsky dramatizes so brilliantly in novels like *Crime and Punishment* and *The Brothers Karamazov*, novels which attempt to estimate the price that must be paid for the freedom he has just discovered. (This theme Nabokov was to explore most exhaustively in *Lolita*.) In the end Albinus must choose between two 'children', his own daughter Irma and Margot. After he chooses the latter, the former soon catches a chill while waiting up for her delinquent father and dies. In one of the novel's most revealing and most powerful scenes, Albinus tries to conjure up memories of Irma but cannot, and decides not to attend his daughter's funeral, so that he can stay and play with his new child.

Of course Albinus's 'freedom' turns out to be the most abject kind of enslavement, he suspects he is being cuckolded but cannot quite prove it, and eventually his murderous jealousy leaves him in the dark quite literally, the victim of an automobile accident that robs him of his sight. His yearning to kill his mistress is linked in complex ways with the other main destructive desire in the novel, the pleasure that the third party in the triangle takes from torturing people. Axel Rex is a gifted artist, but he is also Nabokov's portrait of the artist as sadist. His detachment is not mere lack of compassion, but an obsession with inflicting pain as intense as Albinus's obsession with Margot, and thus he is referred to as Albinus's 'shadow'. Rex sees life as a sort of magic show at which he assists, and the being responsible for the sufferings of someone like Albinus is 'neither God nor the devil' but 'an elusive, double, triple, self-reflecting magic Proteus of a phantom, the shadow of many-colored glass balls flying in a curve, the ghost of a juggler on a shimmering curtain' (124/183). Nabokov often uses such language to describe his ideal novelist, and Axel Rex is a character who turns other people's existence into the black humour of a Nabokov novel. Such explanations of Rex's behaviour tell us nothing very plausible or helpful about his motives: in this novel Nabokov's warning about the psychological approach to character makes more sense. Rex's passing himself off as a homosexual to fool Albinus, the fact that they share a mistress – such details would seem to constitute a *prima facie* case for some homoerotic attraction that is being ruthlessly repressed, but such an explanation would simply loosen the malevolent hold he exercises over the reader.[12] It is Rex's total lack of feeling for Albinus that makes his sadism so eerie, not any disguised or repressed hatred.

As the novel wends its way through a series of self-destructive acts, the conclusion becomes inevitable. Rex will survive, because he is ultimately only the means by which Albinus destroys his own life. There would have been other lovers, other deceptions; Rex merely precipitates the peripeteia because of the intensity of his inhumanity, and his recklessness. Living in the house with Albinus, he constantly tantalizes his victim's preternaturally sensitive hearing by making sounds that startle and confound him. Recent studies of sadism have elaborated the point that Nabokov makes in novelistic terms here. In her book on torture, Elaine Scarry suggests that humiliation and not just pain is the ultimate object of the sadist: the torturer sets out to 'unmake the world' of his victim by making him 'do or say things – and, if possible, believe and desire things, think thoughts – which later [he] will be unable to cope with having done or thought'.[13] Rex's continued torturing of Albinus, even after he has taken practically everything from him, demonstrates his desire to dismantle Albinus's identity. By making him believe the impossible – that Margot is faithful to him, that Rex's dalliance with her was the play-acting of a homosexual – he can destroy him by making his existence untenable after the truth has been rediscovered. Finally discovered by Albinus's brother-in-law, Rex is physically punished for his cruelty, but he drops out of the novel completely at this point. The last battle is to be, not between Albinus and his shadow, but between him and the girl he has wanted to kill from the beginning.

It is fought out in a locked room, Albinus with his strength and determination to satisfy his desire permanently versus Margot's

cunning and vitality. When she successfully wrestles him for the
gun, the language hints at the whole complex mix of egoism and
self-destructive impulse by which Albinus is undone: 'something let
forth a hideous cry, as though a nightmare creature were being
tickled by its nightmare mate' ('as if someone were being tickled,
but worse' in *Kamera Obskura*]) (203/291). When Albinus ends up
shooting himself, his eyes are filled 'with a dazzling glory' (291).
His obsession has fooled him one last time. What he takes to be
an illumination is merely the final darkness; the desire for release
that he indulged in so recklessly is consummated by death in the
nightmare world he created for himself.

Despair is the work that brings together the obsession plot,
the voice, the black humour, the unfeeling cruelty, and the protagonist, isolated by his insanity, whose extraordinary narrative
resourcefulness makes him, at times, sympathetic, even as he tells
a story that clearly reveals him as murderer and a maniac. Hermann
(his patronymic is Karlovich but we never learn his last name) is as
cut off from the real world as Luzhin, as self-deceiving as Smurov,
and as fixated as Albinus, but Nabokov's new protagonist is more
than just a composite because he has been given an eloquence, a
power of articulation, an awareness of himself as literary artist that
makes the novel a more substantial achievement than Nabokov's
early essays in the obsession genre.

Despair consists of the tale of a murder told by the madman
who commits it. Nabokov begins his novel by having his narrator
introduce the metaphor around which the story turns: a crime is
a work of art. Hermann tells us that the sequence of events he has
created in real life, and is now simply transposing, is an index of
his creative genius, and he hints on page one that the sequence
involves a crime for which he is responsible. As our suspicions about
his sanity grow, he attempts to forestall them with comments like
the following:

> A clever Lett whom I used to know in Moscow in 1919 said to
> me once that the clouds of brooding which occasionally and
> without any reason came over me were a sure sign of my ending
> in a madhouse. He was exaggerating, of course; during this last
> year I have thoroughly tested the remarkable qualities of clarity
> and cohesion exhibited by the logical masonry ['architecture' in
> *Otchayanie*] in which my strongly developed, but perfectly normal
> mind indulged. (10–11/18)

The introductory passages and this sort of speech begin to establish the parameters of the strange world *Despair* creates. When Hermann reassures his readers that his mind works logically, he reminds us that he is not mad in at least one sense of the word. As long as reason is thought of as 'the organ of moral perception as well as the ratiocinative faculty',[14] then the idea of someone being both rational and insane makes no sense. But since the Enlightenment, philosophers have driven a wedge between the two notions. Hume remarks in a famous passage: "'Tis not contrary to reason to prefer the destruction of the whole world to the scratching of my little finger'.[15] As A. D. Nuttall points out, 'the sentence is clearer if we italicize "reason"'. He continues:

> The argument is on its own terms entirely sound. And the conclusion is clear. A man who would blow up the world to stop his finger itching is mad. Such a man (we have agreed) is not irrational, makes no error in reasoning. Therefore reason and madness are perfectly compatible.[16]

A man who sets out to rearrange his life by murdering the man he takes to be his double so that he can assume a new identity makes no error in reasoning either; and thus Hermann is Nabokov's first great study in the rational madness that Hume's comment defines.

The novel makes fairly clear that Hermann's 'despair' is occasioned by his wife's faithlessness and his own jealousy; but whereas in *Laughter in the Dark* female infidelity and the passions it arouses are the whole point, in *Despair* Hermann's sexual relations with his wife are only the occasion for a fantasy that locks both him and the reader into the comic divagations of his solipsistic consciousness. Hermann enjoys so much his rôle as a spectator during his nightly lovemaking that he finds himself watching his acting self at ever-increasing distances from the bedroom. He confesses:

> I longed to contemplate that bedroom scene from some remote upper gallery in a blue mist under the swimming allegories of the starry vault; to watch a small but distinct and very active couple through opera glasses, field glasses, a tremendous telescope, or optical instruments of yet unknown power that would grow larger in proportion to my increasing rapture.[17] (38)

Alas, the spectator in Hermann takes over to such an extent that even as he imagines himself to be vigorously making love to his

wife, she asks him to bring her a book since he is not coming
to bed. This breaks the spell, we are told, and it is only a 'new
and wonderful obsession' (39), that is, his discovery of his double,
Felix, that causes him to lose interest in his amatory experiments
altogether. The parallelism is clear: unable to satisfy his wife he
brings her a book, an escapist fantasy – her reading habits are
itemized in contemptuous detail – that provides her with the
vicarious thrills she needs to alleviate her own boredom; unable
to satisfy the world that the man he killed is identical to him, he
offers it a book, his explanation and attempt at justifying his escapist
fantasy as fact.

Thus *Despair* is really two stories told simultaneously, the story of
the murder and the story of the story, Hermann's auto-commentary
on the writing itself. And it is not as if the writing begins when
the action (disastrously) ends; rather, the action catches up with
and overtakes Hermann's story, so that what he finally writes out
while he hides from the police is simply the most elaborate of the
fictions he has created in lieu of actually living. Here, of course,
lies the problem: hopelessly wrapped up in his introspection, he
ultimately finds that it has cut him off from the world altogether.
Instead of meditating on a self, he ends up staring into a mirror at
a face staring at him. The point is relevant to every one of Nabokov's
self-conscious protagonists in that ultimately their obsession with
self makes them all incapable of the self-forgetting necessary to
have a relationship with someone else, or, for that matter, to
arrive at an relatively disinterested sense of what constitutes their
own identity.

As an exercise in literary self-consciousness, *Despair* invokes a
number of authors as precursors. A Pushkin love lyric evokes
Hermann's desire for tranquility ('long have I, weary slave, been
contemplating flight') (60/72),[18] but the allusion echoes ominously, for Pushkin, soon after he wrote his poem, obtained the
tranquility he sought (and satisfaction for his wife's flirtations) by
getting himself killed in a duel. Like one of Browning's murderous
monologists, Hermann wants the peace that comes from mastery,
a desire that is only realizable in the self-created world he inhabits.
He composes an epilogue to his story, one that coyly distributes *à
la* Turgenev the appropriate endings to everyone concerned, only
to dismiss it as sarcastically as he dismisses his wife. But the author
who figures most prominently in the novel is Fyodor Dostoevsky.
The first allusion to his work occurs as Hermann wonders about

the accuracy of a dialogue between him and Felix he has just recounted:

> There is something a shade too literary about that talk of ours, smacking of thumb-screw conversations in those stage taverns where Dostoevski is at home; a little more of it and we should hear that sibilant whisper of false humility, that catch in the breath, those repetitions of incantatory adverbs – and then all the rest of it would come, the mystical trimming dear to that famous writer of Russian thrillers.[19] (85–86/98)

Towards the end of *Despair*, both Dostoevsky and his most famous novel, *Crime and Punishment*, are referred to in similarly derogatory fashion. Nabokov dislikes Dostoevsky's novels because, in his view, they contain too many undramatized general ideas, too much sentimentality, too many clichés, too few finely realized details. In many important ways, their interests as writers are antithetical – particularly in so far as their views on the social obligations of the writer and on stylistic matters are concerned – but the similarities between them are at least as interesting. They both write about solipsists and egocentrics, characters who flinch away from the reality of love, who assert their freedom from convention and find that such assertions often bring not life but death, whose desires often involve them with young girls and make them insanely jealous rivals for their affection, who are fascinated by murder, and so forth.

Here Bakhtin's notion of a 'doubly-oriented or doubly-voiced speech' can be useful both in characterizing the novel and in taking into account just how Dostoevsky and his concerns figure in it. What Bakhtin means by this phrase is best defined in his study of Dostoevsky, *Problems of Dostoevsky's Poetics*, which David Lodge has usefully summarized:

> [Doubly-oriented or doubly-voiced speech] includes all speech which not only refers to something in the world but also refers to another speech act by another addresser. It is divided into several subcategories, of which the most important are stylization, *skaz*, parody and hidden polemic. *Stylization* occurs when the writer borrows another's discourse and uses it for his own purposes – with the same general intention as the original, but in the process casting 'a slight shadow of objectification over

it'. This objectification may be used to establish a distance between the narrator and the implied author, especially when the narrator is an individualized character, perhaps narrating his own story. . . . Stylization is to be distinguished from parody, when another's discourse is borrowed but turned to a purpose opposite to or incongruous with the intention of the original. In both stylization and parody, the original discourse is lexically or grammatically evoked in the text.[20]

Bakhtin goes on to demonstrate just what a master of this doubly-oriented speech Dostoevsky actually is, laying particular emphasis on *Notes from Underground* and *Crime and Punishment*.

Any reading of *Despair* must conjure with a discourse that moves freely between stylization, parody, and hidden polemic. The meaning of the novel depends on the reader's appreciating the distance between the narrator and the implied author: the conventional moral standard, articulated by the latter, clashes with the hypertrophied aestheticism of the former in his approach to human affairs. But the implied author, by mocking the confessional novel, the device of the second self, and the mystery novel, and their practitioners, even while he uses them as devices, sets up another series of doubled discourses. And, of course, Hermann, the self-conscious narrator with literary pretensions, also implicates himself in this matrix by his self-conscious exhibition of narrative and linguistic skills. He is, after all, *the* superior creative artist in the novel (the man who cuckolds him is merely a drunken parasite with some talent). Yet, curiously, this multilevelled structure finally makes the novel seem somehow thinner than anything it parodies in Dostoevsky. The reason for this becomes clearer if we consider the nature of the text that is being parodied. Unlike, say, Tolstoy or George Eliot, Dostoevsky in his major novels

does not rely on already available and stable positions – family, social, biographical . . . All social and cultural institutions, establishments, social states and classes, family relationships, are no more than positions in which a person can be eternally equal to himself.[21]

But whereas Dostoevsky uses this narrative instability to explore spiritual and metaphysical questions and to test the equivocal answers they often provide us, Nabokov's clever mockery of the

whole notion of such a search leaves him only quizzically interested
in pursuing it, and in *Despair* he pushes the questions less far than
his famous precursor as a result.

In the end, the murderer stands condemned, by the police, by his
conduct, by his own conscience. But, as he does in so many of his
novels, Nabokov deliberately leaves the ending open. The last word
in the Russian original of *Despair* is *rech'* (speech), as Hermann
talks to himself about what he should do. Just as he begins his narrative thinking about how to begin, so he ends it with speculations
about how to end it. Nabokov added the 'speech' to the English
version, and it too is a non-ending, a proposal for a movie starring
Hermann in the rôle of escape artist, with the crowd obligingly
preventing the police from arresting him. The point is that the
book need not end with his arrest because his speech cannot be
arrested. Bahktin describes the openness at the end of Dostoevsky's
novels this way: 'nothing conclusive has yet taken place in the
world, the ultimate word of the world and about the world has
not yet been spoken, the world is open and free, everything is still
in the future and will always be in the future'.[22] Nabokov in effect
parodies this catharsis: the openness in Dostoevsky points to social
and political possibilities yet unrealized; the openness at the end of
Despair reminds us that Hermann's social vision is simply a parodic
post hoc justification for his crime ('This remarkable physical like-
ness probably appealed to me [subconsciously!] as the promise of
that ideal sameness which is to unite people in the classless society
of the future' [150–51/168]), which Hermann wryly includes as the
net closes in on him. Dostoevsky refuses to say the last word because
he believes that social reform is possible. Nabokov refuses to say it
because he wants that voice to go on resonating in our heads, long
after we have solemnly made all the correct ethical judgements and
banished Hermann to his own private hell.

These four novels of obsession, as well as offering distinctive pleasures of their own, constitute a sort of quadripartite propaedeutic
for the fiction that follows. In teaching us to read Nabokov's later
work, they show how his engagement with narrative resulted in the
creation of a device, the obsession plot, that enables him to explore
the self-reflexive world of narrative, the skewed psychology that so
fascinates him, the tension between the energy of the egocentric
and the lacunae his solipsism occasions, and the recognition that
the obsessive intensity that makes people pretty awful human
beings, because it tends to obscure their sense of other people's

existence, can make them curiously gifted in other ways. In the next chapter, we shall see how he experimented with fictional forms that freed him from the mimetic obligations imposed upon him by both the autobiographical fiction and the novels of obsession. He had a mixed success in his search for a new mode, but it facilitated his transition into a new language, and led to the major achievements of the 1950s and 1960s.

4

Experiments in Mid-Career: *Invitation to a Beheading, The Real Life of Sebastian Knight,* and *Bend Sinister*

From the middle of the 1930s, Nabokov's fiction became more overtly experimental, as he worked to find a form appropriate for the nightmare worlds he saw developing around him, and as he made the shift from Russian to English. His penultimate Russian novel, *Invitation to a Beheading*, and the first two novels in his new language, *The Real Life of Sebastian Knight* and *Bend Sinister*, show not only that Nabokov had the skill and the range to innovate in mid-career, but also that he could depict sensitivity and compassion as convincingly as he could cruelty and pain, and that the problematic ways in which language creates and presents a self continue to be his main subject.

Invitation to a Beheading is a very spare book that threatens to end almost as soon as it begins, since we learn in the first paragraph that its hero as been sentenced to death:

So we are nearing the end. The right-hand, still untasted part of the novel, which, during our delectable reading, we would lightly feel, mechanically testing whether there were still plenty left (and our fingers were always gladdened by the placid, faithful thickness), had suddenly, for no reason at all, become quite

meagre: a few minutes of quick reading, already downhill, and
– O horrible! (26/12)

The passage invites us to consider the various ways in which text
and world can be conflated. E. M. Forster once pointed out that
if it were not for wedding bells and funerals the novelist would
hardly know where to stop; that is, novels rely on certain conventional endings which we come to expect in the appropriate places.
Nabokov announces here that he is going to expose the arbitrary
nature of such conventions: books are not obliged to contain well
ordered lives conveyed in great detail, and much of the novel plays
with the humour that results from the reader's puzzlement at the
consequent reordering that takes place.

Other conventions are toyed with and discarded. Readers are
lured into thinking that *Invitation to a Beheading* might be a prison
narrative in which the victim fights his jailors, tries to escape,
engages the help of his relatives, petitions his judges, confronts
his executioner, and so on. But though Cincinnatus C., the hero,
does indeed try all of these things, they are revealed in the course of
the novel to be the wrong way out for him, and a trap for those who
did not recognize them as the hackneyed conventions of adventure
stories. Nabokov wants the reader to compare the task that the hero
is attempting to perform with his or her own task: that is, both are
confronted by certain signs which can be interpreted in a number
of ways; both are eager to understand these signs so that they can
figure out exactly what kind of world they find themselves in; both
are frustrated by false leads, misleading associations, and erroneous
conclusions; both arrive at the end with a partial understanding of
what they have experienced, an understanding that can conceivably
be put to use for other texts, other lives. Psychological, political,
and gnostical readings of the events form plausible parts of the
larger picture, but the emphasis always returns to the act of reading
that Nabokov foregrounds at the outset.

Cincinnatus is to be executed because he has been found guilty
of being 'a lone dark obstacle in this world of souls transparent
to one another' (36/24), and that is all the novel says about
his crime. In Nabokov's view, a Russian *émigré* writing in the
1930s should not need to say any more: the oppressiveness of
Soviet totalitarianism was patently obvious and represented the
inevitable tendency of totalitarian governments everywhere. He is
not interested in exploring in his novels why certain governments

tyrannize their populations, or what the social consequences of
such actions are. They simply do it, and that makes them stupid
and cruel and figures of fun. The robust, no-nonsense quality of this
particular view of the question is certainly attractive, and the great
advantage of such a position is the comic capital he can make of it.
Thus he concentrates on the absurdities of the prison regime, the
arrangements for the execution, the boorish appetites and habits
of those who surround the prisoner. The prison has rules banning
certain kinds of dreams, the management refuses to take responsibility 'for the loss of property or of the inmate himself' (60/49), the
prison director and his underlings enjoy frequent intercourse with
the (perfectly willing) wife of the prisoner – in other words, having
defined an ideal situation for black humour, Nabokov exploits it
to the full. The disadvantage is that Cincinnatus's persecutors are
ultimately more silly than menacing. If one comes to the novel
looking for something resembling the insight into the nature of
ordered tyranny that one finds in Zamyatin's *We*, or the analysis of
the tension between a deep-seated human need for genuine culture
and the delights of a soothing blend of order and illusion that
constitutes Huxley's *Brave New World*, or the study of the psychology
of the Stalinist victim that informs Koestler's *Darkness at Noon*, or
the depiction of the ways totalitarianism dehumanizes its victims in
Orwell's *Nineteen Eighty-Four*, then one will go away disappointed.

The writer most likely to come to readers' minds in regard to
Invitation is Kafka. The puzzled protagonist, desperately trying to
understand what is happening to him and why, the dogged battle
between the sharply defined individual and his faceless persecutors,
the nightmare setting that compounds his difficulties by its very
mobility, its propensity or frustrating his attempts to acquire knowledge by taking on the dynamic qualities he manifests in his attempt
to escape it – these similarities are certainly important. Yet Nabokov
denied having any knowledge of Kafka's work at the time he wrote
the novel, and generally resented being compared to other writers.
Here I think Nabokov is in one sense correct: he and Kafka are in
many ways completely opposed as writers, but the very difference
between them is itself illuminating.

Consider the following scene from an early chapter in which the
prisoner is led to the top of his prison to gaze out at the landscape:

> one could distinguish the traffic moving on First Boulevard, and
> an amethystine shimmer at the end, where the famous fountain

played; and still further, toward the hazy folds of the hills that
formed the horizon, there was the dark stipple of oak groves,
with, here and there, a pond gleaming like a hand mirror,
while other bright ovals of water gathered, glowing through
the tender mist, over there to the west, where the serpentine
Strop had its source. Cincinnatus, his palm pressed to his cheek,
in motionless, ineffably vague and perhaps even blissful despair,
gazed at the glimmer and haze of the Tamara Gardens and at
the dove-blue melting hills beyond them – oh, it was a long time
before he could take his eyes away . . . .

'How bewitching all this is', said Cincinnatus, addressing the
gardens, the hills (and for some reason it was especially pleasant
to repeat the word 'bewitching' in the wind, somewhat as children cover and then expose their ears, amused at this renewal
of the audible world). (37–38)

The key phrases here are 'ineffably vague' and 'blissful despair',
the first denoting that feeling that so often wafts over the Nabokov
hero when some important sign is there to be decoded, the second
an apparent oxymoron that suggests the purely temporary quality
of Cincinnatus's situation: he can experience bliss in his despair
because the scene he surveys denotes all the magical qualities of
the world into which he longs to escape, into which he will escape as
soon as he realizes that his servitude is self-imposed. Such moments
occur in Kafka, but there they are ironized, subject to the same
qualifications and constraints that always characterize his darker
worlds. Cincinnatus can escape, the world beyond the prison really
is this alluring; whereas Kafka's heroes must recognize the world as
their prison and escape as impossible. Cincinnatus tries to escape,
must escape, because he is innocent. In Kafka's work, the hero feels
guilty because his creator does. Kafka once wrote in his diary: 'This
morning, after a long time, I again took pleasure in imagining that
a knife is turned in my heart'; and he talked about the 'bliss' in
'welcoming, with so deep a sense of freedom, conviction and joy,
the punishment when it came'.[1]

In addition, the critical free play afforded by Kafka's texts is
different in kind from the injunctions Nabokov offers us. Good
and bad, intelligence and stupidity, the genuine and the false –
in this novel Nabokov wants his readers to have a secure sense of
these distinctions. When Martha copulates with the prison director,
we know that she is another risible Nabokovian subhuman, trapped

in a body that constitutes her entire presence in the non-world of base desire, a grotesque parody of the unfaithful wife. When the executioner literally shrinks away to nothing at the end of the novel, and all the characters become as unreal and devoid of interest as the pieces of flapping scenery, this merely confirms what we have known about them, in moral terms, from the beginning. As they disappear, Cincinnatus moves in a certain direction 'where, to judge by the voices, stood beings akin to him' (218/223), we know it is a positive one. For all his feints and duplicitous strategies, Nabokov inevitably instils in the reader the confidence necessary to make such discriminations, and this tendency is a direct result of the confidence with which he makes them.

Throughout the course of the novel Cincinnatus is trying to write something, to express something ineffable. His attempts to write it out are frustrated by the nature of language itself: 'will nothing come of what I am trying to tell', he muses at one point, 'its only vestiges being the corpses of strangled words, like hanged men . . . evening silhouettes of gammas and gerunds, gallow crows'.[2] The brilliant play with the gallows shapes of the old Church Slavonic characters here is lost in the translation, but the notion of the writer's task as transcribing something that exists beyond words returns repeatedly in different guises in the Russian novels. (Nabokov once said in an interview: 'I know more than I can express in words, and the little I can express would not have been expressed, had I not know more'.)[3] What distinguishes Cincinnatus from the non-beings around him is precisely his awareness of this other world to which his imagination gives access. The world that he longs for is variously associated with the innocence of children, pastoral settings, bodilessness, effortless pleasure, in short, the standard reveries of the romantic imagination at idle. But Nabokov sharpens the image a little in the one moment at which Cincinnatus comes closest to realizing that, spiritually linked to his creator's active imagination, he does belong to a different order, that if lives can end as books begin, so too can they begin as books end.

The moment occurs in the interview between him and his mother. Its parodic, conventional status is prepared for by the absurdities and wild humour that characterize every other interview Cincinnatus has, with his wife, with his relatives, with the prison officials, and in particular the grotesque and hilarious series with his own executioner during which 'M'sieur Pierre' (the French in the novel denotes the phoney gentility used to mask torture and cruelty) tries to establish some sort of intimate link with his proposed victim. All these prepare the reader for more black humour when she appears, but her visit differs in a couple of important respects. Parental links are nearly always quasi-sacred things in Nabokov's novels, and even Cincinnatus's prodigal parents are no exception. First of all his mother brings the important news that his father was also 'opaque'; that is, there are 'beings akin' to Cincinnatus in the world somewhere. Then she indicates another kind of kinship by talking about how hard she is working at 'expressing something', exactly like her son labouring away at his last testament. She tells a story about some 'nonnons', grotesque and shapeless objects turned by a special mirror into 'wonderful, sensible images', and as she concludes her strange story Cincinnatus notices something in her eyes:

> it was as if something real, unquestionable (in this world, where everything was subject to question), had passed through, as if a corner of this horrible life had curled up, and there was a glimpse of the lining. In his mother's gaze, Cincinnatus suddenly saw that ultimate, secure, all-explaining and from-all-protecting spark that he knew how to discern in himself also. What was this spark so piercingly expressing now? It does not matter what – call it horror, or pity . . . .

This image of the turned up corner, the glimpse of the lining, is one that recurs in similar situations – in *The Gift*, in *Speak, Memory* – when the irony markers disappear for a moment, and the words point towards something whose existence is not the less certain for being so difficult to express. As always, it connotes a capacity for feeling and its existence is limited to the special few whose humanity distinguishes them from the harsh and envious group of simulacra surrounding them. Cincinnatus's mother is a midwife: that is, she eases the transition between worlds (the executioner grotesquely parodies her rôle). Thus when she leaves her son, she makes the midwife's gesture, 'holding her hands with index fingers apart, as if indicating size – the length, say, of a babe (138/136). Nabokov wants us to recall here the 'ancient and enigmatic' graffiti on the wall of Cincinnatus's cell: 'Measure me while I live – after it will be too late' (39/26; the play on words in the first phrase, 'Smer'te do smerti, is lost in the translation). Cincinnatus has been

duly measured; birth and not death awaits him when he awakes
from his nightmare.

The ending announces the proud independence of the individual confident enough to impose his own vision on reality, or
the unbending courage of the victim in the face of outrageous
persecution – Soviet, Nazi – that ennobles him even as he fearfully,
innocently goes to his death, or the moment at which the spirit,
fighting free of its earthly chains, becomes one with the more
real reality its very existence confirms. *Invitation to a Beheading* will
support all these and other readings, yet the most all-encompassing
account would seem to be the one that takes us back to the idea of
the book as the artefact in which such syntheses can take place.
Cincinnatus has his strange fulfilment; the author expresses his
vision; readers experience cognate thrills and frustrations on the
way to that moment at the end when the book reveals itself as both
text and world.

The Real Life of Sebastian Knight is another novel written during
the crucial transitional period in Nabokov's life when he changed
languages and countries. And, in its very different way, it too is
about how experience can be transposed into words, and about
the different orders of reality that such transpositions suggest. This
time Nabokov's questing hero is known to us only by an initial,
V., and the problem he must solve is on the surface much more
mundane than the one Cincinnatus C. faces: he wants to write a
biography of his half brother, the 'real life' referred to in the title.
Yet the self-effacement represented by that single letter, and the
complications that ensue when V. tries to sort out the details from
the life of a person he hardly knew, suggest that the complexities
involved in any attempt to present a self in language are Nabokov's
chief subject once again. Just as Cincinnatus is constantly being
reprimanded for his refusal to speak in the language of 'the
other' – his rudeness and bluntness are manifestations of his
rejection of accepted formulae that cover up a hideous reality –
so too does V. stumble again and again on the problems involved
in using the narrative conventions of biography in his account
of his brother's life. By foregrounding the conflation of life and
literary art, by arranging for the reader's quest to mimic the
narrator's as he did in *Invitation*, Nabokov goes to work again
on the problems of fiction-making that preoccupied him during
this period.

In his illuminating study of the biography as a form, Ira Nadel summarizes the 'set of paradigms that organize the representation of lives' as

> (1) the idea that a biography is a history of an individual, functioning as a record or commemoration of a life; (2) the idea that a biography presents an example, a model of moral and didactic value for readers; (3) the idea that biography is discovery, revealing previously unknown aspects of the subject often through detail or anecdote.[4]

Nadel adds that aesthetic reasons can be as important in the genesis of a biography as historical ones, and that 'discovery in biography now exists equally in what the biographer reveals about himself as well as in what he uncovers about his subject'. These five points neatly encapsulate V's project in this novel. The first three are what he tries to do. He wants to write his book as an act of homage or commemoration for an unjustly forgotten novelist. The value of this exercise for its readers will be an account of the exemplary life lived by this fiercely independent artist. His secret love, the subject of V.'s quest throughout much of the book, will be discovered by interviews, documents, and the detective-style sleuthing necessary to get at the heart of any mystery. But the two addenda occasioned by the changing form of twentieth-century narrative dictate the actual course his book is to take. The chronological approach to his material gradually yields to one which gives priority to Sebastian Knight's own fiction, and the account of V.'s investigation along with its surprising conclusion tells us at least as much about the biographer as it does about its subject.

We learn early on that V. has a rival, one Mr. Goodman who has already written a biography of this strange writer. Mr. Goodman is insensitive to Sebastian's special genius, primarily because he conveys the historical background of his subject's life in a series of dismal clichés. As we have already seen, the idea that anyone might be 'a product of his time' fills Nabokov with loathing, since his notion of individuality precludes the nebulous passivity implied by such a phrase. Sebastian has what Cincinnatus has: 'his slightest thought or sensation had always at least one more dimension than those of his neighbours' (66); he is 'a crystal among glass'. Those who fail to see this are the enemy, and they are finally as disposable as Cincinnatus's persecutors. Goodman is a bit of a straw man in this regard, although he is handy as a summary-type portrayal of everything that Nabokov believes is inimical to genuine writing. V'.s biography, if it is to convey the essence of this man's life must find both the details and the language that convey its subject's uniqueness.

A better though rather trickier way of getting at the real life of this particular author turns out to be through his books. For those who have encountered in preface after preface Nabokov's insistence that his own fiction must never be used in this way, the proposition may seem rather odd, but as we shall see there is no real contradiction here. After V.'s attempts to discover information from various human contacts prove relatively unsuccessful, he begins to summarize Sebastian's novels. We learn that in his first, as a protest against the conventionality of second-rate authors, he has written 'a rollicking parody' and 'a wicked imitation' of a detective novel. The actual excerpts from *The Prismatic Bezel* make it sound rather less rollicking and wicked than V. would have us believe, but Nabokov's point is that the secret of Sebastian's success resides in his formal innovation. Just as modes of representation in painting have changed radically in this century, so too have the narrative modes in the novel. Since biography is inextricably bound up with the biographer's choice of storytelling strategies, and also owes its methods of characterization to what it has learned from the novel, V. can write the 'real life' of his subject by using his fiction, not as a collection of *romans à clef*, but as a source for his own techniques. The heroes of Sebastian's detective novel are called 'methods of composition' (95), because in it he seeks to convey a way of seeing rather than the essence of a personality. V. must attempt to do the same.

In this sense, *The Real Life of Sebastian Knight* seems to anticipate the claims of literary theorists who propose 'the tactical elimination of the whole idea of a safe, securable, person-like source of writing, a creative individual who is the only true begetter and valid first cause of the literary text. . . . They tell us that writers do not so much write as get written, that it is not authors who construct books but readers, and that the only true object of attention is text as language'.[5] Yet although such critics often cite Nabokov in passing when advancing such arguments, this particular novel offers only partial support for these propositions about authorship. Sebastian Knight is indeed elusive, but not because his books have been written to illustrate the Death of the Author and the Death of the Subject, the non-existence of an authentic ego which is responsible for making and having 'a life'. Sebastian exists all right, it is just that the conventional means of imposing a shape on that existence – interviewing friends and acquaintances, tracking down different accounts of relationships, examining letters and documents – leads to a series of comic dead ends.

The summary of Sebastian's next book, *Success*, reveals it to be a recapitulation of the 'fate' theme that so intrigues Nabokov in his own life, and in novels as different as *Laughter in the Dark*, *The Gift*, and *Lolita*. He routinely elevates chance and coincidence into vaguely mystical, deeply significant forces which strongly hint at some shaping power with certain aesthetic ends in mind. But the most important thing we learn about *Success* is that there is a conjuror who figures prominently in it. This character is introduced because he is about to make a appearance in V'.s life, in the form of a Mr. Silbermann he meets on a train. V. is looking for a mysterious woman whom Sebastian pursued just before he died, and he needs a list of the women who stayed at a resort hotel where Sebastian met her one summer. Silbermann expresses his sorrow for Sebastian's death, agrees to help and magically produces the list, but advises V. that the pursuit of this woman is useless. Like Cincinnatus's mother, what Sebastian's creation has to offer is compassion, and he fears that V. will exploit the information for his own private ends. At this point V. has not understood the conflation of worlds that has occurred, but the mode of payment for the favours Mr. Silbermann performs makes clear that V. has grasped one lesson: after a complicated exchange of various sums, no money actually changes hands, but V. promises to thank him in his book. With this remark he implies that if his mysterious helper reads *Sebastian Knight*, Silbermann will find there the same sort of compassion, the same reluctance to pry into the secrets of the dead, the same metaphoric identification between man and book, real life and fiction, that he exemplified in his dealings with V.

Not only do fictional characters pop into existence to play Virgil to V.'s Dante, thus disorienting readers who are used to the fictions mentioned in their fiction staying separate from it, but there are other sources of confusion as well. Nabokov himself (deliberately?) confuses readers by forcing them to ask continuously 'Who is speaking?' Consider the following description of Sebastian Knight:

> he belonged to that rare type of writer who knows that nothing ought to remain except the perfect achievement: the printed

book; that its actual existence is inconsistent with that of its spectre, the uncouth manuscript flaunting its imperfections like a revengeful ghost carrying its own head under its arm; and that for this reason the litter of the workshop, no matter its sentimental or commercial value, must never subsist. (36)

The sort of public a New Directions novel like *Sebastian Knight* might appeal to were no doubt puzzled by the supposedly non-literary narrator's pronouncing on such matters. Not because they had not been exposed to the complexities of modernist texts, but rather because they had. The elusive intricacies of Conrad, Bely, or Faulkner often make for a very elaborate sort of narrative complexity, but these do not include allowing characters to speak out of character. Modernism was not gratuitous disorder, as some of its early critics claimed, but a discipline that required readers to learn a new set of rules by which to judge fiction. In this novel Nabokov makes his own rules, and simply flouts the convention that confines a character's opinions to areas in which he can be assumed to have a certain competence.

The rest of *Sebastian Knight* consists of a teasing series of hints and guesses about various identities, and sly suggestions about various possibilities that readers are forced to entertain: that V. successfully finds his way through the thicket of clues obscuring the identity of the woman Sebastian loved; that Sebastian's shade assists his half-brother by easing him into the evanescent world of a novelist's imaginings; that V'.s obsession with his brother takes him into a nightmare world in which his goal recedes even as he seems to be drawing near it; that the whole book is a fictitious biography dreamed up by Sebastian himself, populated by characters from all his novels. The casual, intermittent symbolic suggestions in the book make it possible to defend any one of these readings, and this openness to interpretive possibilities too reminds us of *Invitation*.

But the main point of this exercise in the attempted re-creation of another's life remains clear. As Sebastian's last novel ends, says V.:

We feel that we are on the brink of some absolute truth, dazzling in its splendour and at the same time almost homely in its perfect simplicity. By an incredible feat of suggestive wording, the author makes us believe that he knows the truth about death and that he is going to tell it. . . the intricate pattern of human life

turns out to be monogrammatic, now quite clear to the inner eye
disentangling the interwoven letters. And the word, the meaning
which appears is astounding in its simplicity: the greatest surprise
being perhaps that in the course of one's earthly existence, with
one's brain encompassed by an iron ring, by the close-fitting
dream of one's own personality – one had not made by chance
that simple mental jerk, which would have set free imprisoned
thought and granted it the great understanding. (178–79)

All of this should be familiar territory for readers by now: the
dualism that gestures towards a world in which, unencumbered by
the flesh, the soul assumes its natural contours; the arbitrariness of
the personality one adopts in the earthly phase of one's existence;
the idea of life as a lyrical mystery that death somehow solves; the
centrality of language (the word, the monogram) in any conception of how this transcendental signifier might present itself.

The conclusion of Sebastian's novel anticipates the conclusion
of V.'s, in which he announces that he *has* been granted the great
understanding, discovered the arbitrariness of personality, and
conceived the book as the means by which this transformation can
best be conveyed. As in *Invitation*, the moment of the revelation is
prepared for by a mock death scene. V. rushes to the bedside of his
dying half brother, and communes with him by listening from an
adjoining room to the rhythm of his breathing:

> The strange dream I had had, the belief in some momentous
> truth he would impart to me before dying – now seemed vague,
> abstract, as if it had been drowned in some warm flow of simpler,
> more human emotion, in the wave of love I felt for the man who
> was sleeping beyond that half-opened door. (202–3)

But this profound link turns out to be a feint designed to dupe
those who are, like V., given to sentimental excess. This man who
has more or less ignored him his whole life is not to be embraced in
a conventional death-bed scene, and saved by the heroic last-minute
ministrations of his half brother. On leaving the room, V. learns
that he has been visiting someone else, that Sebastian died the
night before, that life has played another joke on him. The point
is twofold, I think. Firstly, the warm love V. imagines is earthbound,
since it depends on some kind of human exchange, and secondly,
Nabokov loves to mock his own characters when they imagine that

they have guessed a secret or discovered a truth, particularly when that secret or that truth hints at the existence of a world that transcends this one.

Yet, as in *Invitation,* in another sense the 'death' of the hero of the book simply does not matter:

> Whatever his secret was, I have learnt one secret too, and namely: that the soul is but a manner of being – not a constant state – that any soul may be yours, if you find and follow its undulations. The hereafter may be the full ability of consciously living in any chosen soul, in any number of souls, all of them unconscious of their interchangeable burden. (204–5)

V. then announces that he *is* Sebastian Knight, and he concludes the book with a vision of all the characters from Sebastian's life around him on a lighted stage. The wording and the context make clear that he is 'impersonating' his half-brother, that his act of sympathetic identification has reached some sort of completion here, that these are not the closing remarks of the real Sebastian, who has all the time been pretending to be a non-existent person. As a truth about how character works in a Nabokov novel, it reminds us that the 'modes of composition' we have responded to are simply nodes in the texture of the work, that a novel that moves as freely between levels of reality as this one reveals the arbitrariness of an author's decisions about the method to proceed. As a truth about the limitations imposed on any biographer by his medium, the concluding passage is equally suggestive. Nadel remarks that the 'double bind' of biography is the 'conflict that results from the effort to merge the actual and imagined individual', and concludes: 'Its task of reconstructing while deconstructing intensifies the difficulty of its factual and literary natures. Language, however, mediates the problem, especially metaphor'. The whole passage serves as an admirable gloss of Nabokov's project in this novel, and the last point is crucial for an understanding of the ending and of Nabokov's approach to the nature of language itself.

The metaphors at the end of *Sebastian Knight* – the monogram, the prison, the interchangeable soul, the stage – constitute the controlling tropes of Sebastian's life. The monogram is a sign that links him to the half-brother who presents himself to us as one; the prison is the body from which the soul escapes whenever it is required to take imaginative flight; the interchangeable soul is the fluidity of identity which the creative artist's negative capability makes possible; the stage is the fiction in which as author he assumes his various rôles. What V. has done in the process of researching his biography is shape his own understanding of his subject, and located that understanding on the edge of the ineffable, that area of language in which metaphor locates us. Unable to discover the contiguous, linear, horizontal narrative he sought, he told the story of his frustration, and in doing so created the circular, vertical account that ends, not by announcing a discursive truth but by imparting an imaginative one.

Commenting on the novel later, Nabokov spoke of its 'unbearable imperfections',[6] perhaps because he initially conceived the novel as a carefully arranged series of ironic undercuttings of V.'s bumblingly solemn search, and thought he'd wandered too far from his main theme, perhaps because he thought the ending too sentimental or too simplistic. If one has a somewhat pompous fool as a narrator, one can have a great deal of fun at his expense, but V. has to do double duty as comic figure and as someone who makes fun of those who are much less sensitive than he (yet the protagonist of *Lolita* performs both rôles with no particular sign of strain). The confusion of fictional realms at the end also contributes to the diffuse, unfocused quality which characterizes this novel, as it does no other Nabokov wrote. In *The Eye* the confusion about the hero's identity is a product of his insecurities, not the author's divided purpose; in *Invitation to a Beheading*, levels of reality are conflated at the end but the story makes it clear to us readers which one we should dismiss. In *Sebastian Knight*, Nabokov made interesting aesthetic capital out of his own apparent indecision, and then proceeded to judge himself more harshly than did the critics who took the lack of focus to be intentional.

Bend Sinister represents the third of the novels written by Nabokov to test the limits of the genre on which he had already made such a mark. Again he presents us with a solitary figure who must face up to questions about human mortality, about the conflation of the fictive and the real, about the role of language as creative distraction in an oppressive world. Like Cincinnatus, Adam Krug, a proud, independent philosopher in a Central European country governed by a despotic mediocrity, is contemptuous of those who would force him to conform because he is different. Like V., he is searching for a secret that imposes some kind of transcendent meaning on human suffering. And as in both *Invitation to a Beheading* and *The Real Life of Sebastian Knight,* in *Bend Sinister* Nabokov is acutely conscious of his rôle as 'anthropomorphic deity', manipulating events and projecting himself into the world of the novel at crucial points.

In the Introduction, the most helpful commentary he wrote on any of his novels, Nabokov insists that twentieth-century politics had only a negligible influence on the novel, that he has no political statement to make in it, and that, instead of such matters, human tenderness, patterns of images and linguistic play should preoccupy the careful reader. The overstatement here is deliberate and provocative, but this sort of stage direction obviously links *Bend Sinister* to its predecessors, in which Nabokov uses the tension between the ostensible content and the formal innovations he experiments with to write a new kind of novel.

Bend Sinister opens with Krug watching a scene from a window, concentrating on its details so that he will not have to think about the fact that his wife is dying, and this split prefigures the split with Krug himself:

> As usual he discriminated between the throbbing one and the one that looked on: looked on with concern, with sympathy, with a sigh, or with bland surprise. This was the last stronghold of the dualism he abhorred. . . . In every mask I tried on, there were slits for his eyes. Even at the very moment when I was rocked by the convulsion men value most. My saviour. My witness. (7)

Krug may abhor his own dualism, but, like every Nabokov hero, he is stuck with it, and is forced to use a language that has men 'value' their sexual 'convulsions' as a result. And he feels it even more acutely because his corporeal world is peopled by the grossest and cruellest sort of animals posing as human beings. Having survived an encounter with some soldiers on his return from the hospital, he thinks about the difference between him and them:

> He remembered other imbeciles he and she had studied, a study conducted with a kind of gloating enthusiastic disgust. Men who got drunk on beer in sloppy bars, the process of thought satisfactorily replaced by swine-toned radio music. Murderers. The respect a business magnate evokes in his home town. Literary critics praising the books of their friends or partisans. Flaubertian *farceurs.* Fraternities, mystic orders. People who are amused by trained animals. The members of reading clubs. All

those who *are* because they do *not* think, thus refuting Cartesianism. The thrifty peasant. The booming politician. (11)

Disgust and contempt in Nabokov are always concomitant with tenderness: the more intensely his characters feel about their wives or lovers or children, the more comprehensively they repudiate those in the world whom that feeling excludes. People in groups and people whose lives are clichés are always a threat in his novels, because their limited intellectual capacity and suspect emotional control make them candidates for mob violence of the kind sanctioned by the state in which Krug now lives. The point is underlined by including the inane conversations of such characters, and suturing them together with narrative clichés, in italics: '"Yes, go", said Pietro, *who had overheard the last words*' (14). All these qualities that denote the less than fully human are laid out on an immense axis, to which the narrative will attach the appropriate coefficient of moral opprobrium.

Krug goes that night to a meeting of the university faculty, and although all the events of the early chapters are mediated through his consciousness, he is presented to us at this meeting as if for the first time:

The strong compact dusky forehead had that peculiar hermetic aspect (a bank safe? a prison wall?) which the brows of thinkers possess. The brain consisted of water, various chemical compounds and a group of highly specialized fats. The pale steely eyes were half closed in their squarish orbits under the shaggy eyebrows which had protected them once from the poisonous droppings of extinct birds – Schneider's hypothesis. (47)

The reason for quoting such passages at length becomes obvious when we contrast them to a simple plot summary of the events in this chapter. If one says that Krug, fighting back the grief caused by his wife's death, meets with his colleagues but refuses to save the university by signing a document that indicates his support for the regime, then one has supplied an accurate account of what happens. But this particular event, so important for the rest of the story, which comprises the attempts of the regime to make him comply, is much less memorable than the weird riot of pedantic description, as in the passage above. Its Lombroso-style conclusions about physiognomy and its general mock-scientific specificity poke gentle fun at all the detailed descriptions used to introduce characters in nineteenth-century novels, as well as mocking the pseudo-learning of scientific experts generally, while its comedy deflects our attention from the sordid events being depicted.

The chapter ends with Krug's return home, where he sees a young couple embracing and reflects:

> Cepheus and Cassiopeia in their eternal bliss, and the dazzling tear of Capella, and Polaris the snowflake on the grizzly fur of the Cub, and the swooning galaxies – those mirrors of infinite space *qui m'effrayent, Blaise,* as they did you, and where Olga is not, but where mythology stretches strong circus nets, lest thought, in its ill-fitting tights, should break its old neck instead of rebouncing with a hep and a hop . . . . (61)

Here is the same soaring excess, this time enlisted to reproduce in language the emotional turmoil, the flights of fancy, the repressed desire, the effortless erudition, that help to characterize Krug. His mind seeks desperate solace in the images it conjures up, the bliss of marital immortality from Greek legend, but Cepheus and Cassiopeia are forced to offer their child Andromeda to the gods as a sacrifice; that is, they purchased their eternal bliss with earthly torment, and this constitutes a warning for Krug as well. Pascal's name is invoked, not only because his 'The heart has reasons the mind knows nothing of' is exactly the kind of sentiment the philosopher in Krug would respond to, but also because his metaphysical rigorousness was in part a product of his scientific training. Pascal confesses to being terrified by the infinite emptiness of space, a space that in our century became larger and more empty by a factor of a billion billion or so with the discovery of the existence of galaxies beyond the Milky Way, among which Andromeda was correctly identified for the first time. The circus metaphor invoked at the end continues for almost half a page, and prefigures all Krug's attempts to use mental acrobatics to save himself from the abyss of grief and solitude that constantly threatens to open up before him.

In the next chapter we learn about the origins of the present regime, and the 'Ekwilism' that serves as its official credo. The satire here is directed at two distinct objects: a philosophy that purports to have discovered the potential equality of every citizen, and at the group of people who attempt to impose their version of this 'discovery'. Ekwilism attempts to do for consciousness what Christianity offered in the form of a heavenly paradise and Marxism in the form of an earthly one, an equal measure for all. Nabokov mocks here the extravagance and eccentricity that inevitably occur whenever an exclusive and pedantic rationalism is let loose on the world. Old Skotoma's doctrine constitutes a travesty rather than a parody since 'the humour remains fairly broad, but it is a travesty used for serious purposes. The treatment of Paduk and his group, the ones who eventually seize control of the state, is equally sketchy. Nabokov's revolutionaries are physical and emotional misfits whose rise to power is absurd and inexplicable. Krug has propounded a theory of history which denies that inductive logic can be of any help whatsoever for those who seek to discover historical trends or patterns, and Paduk's rebellion 'proves' it. The concatenation of widespread material deprivation, a revolutionary intelligentsia, and a weak central government that tends to produce upheavals like the one engineered by Paduk are of no novelistic interest to Nabokov, however much they may have affected his own life. He suffered for years from the first and never gave the least thought to overthrowing the governments in power in Berlin and France respectively; he regards the second item in the list as an oxymoron; the third he experienced at first hand in Russia during the reign of Kerensky's Provisional Government and in Germany during the Weimar Republic, but, being temperamentally allergic to such things, Nabokov would never 'corrupt' his fiction with an analysis of the composition or nature of such a government.

Although this makes for certain limitations in the satiric scope of the novel (limitations which Nabokov and many of his readers would refuse to regard as such), it does draw attention to one of the ways in which Nabokov's comedy functions. Think again about Nabokov's dualism, his distinctly patrician ghosts in plebian machines, the mock-scientific description of Krug, the mock-philosophic attempt to forestall grief by using the circus as a metaphor for the universe, the play with rationalism gone wild. Just as those steeped in a certain tradition – Rabelais, Pope, Swift – used the Renaissance view of a unified cosmos to extend the comic possibilities of what they wrote, so too does Nabokov use his own version of the harmonious world they imagined for the patterns on which his novel is based. Galen's physiology, which they used as the basis for their conception of man, has long since been superseded by modern medical science, but practically every character in *Bend Sinister* is as crude a combination of body and soul as anything they imagined. Like Galen's conception, Nabokov's has the advantage of being easy to visualize. His penchant for including meticulously observed detail along with his hyperbolic fantasies also links him with Rabelais, Pope and Swift. In short, Nabokov's novel places him firmly in the tradition of learned wit, and various aspects of the novel are illuminated when seen in this particular light.[7]

For example, most of Chapter Seven is devoted to an outrageous interpretation of *Hamlet* in which Fortinbras emerges as the hero. The reading has all sorts of Fascistic, anti-Semitic overtones ('some base trick on the part of degenerate feudalism, some Masonic manœuvre engendered by the Shylocks of high finance, has dispossessed his family of their just claims' [109]), and Krug's friend Ember must advise the State theatre on how to stage the new version. Everyone acquainted with Krug is being rounded up by the state (Ember is to be next), and to alleviate the tension and stress both men concoct a farrago of nonsensical free association about *Hamlet* and how it might be presented. In such passages, what Pope does to shoddy verse-making in 'The Art of Sinking in Poetry' Nabokov does to a certain type of impressionistic criticism. The flexibility of learned wit in moving back and forth between the flippant and the serious serves him well in such passages. For the reader in search of psychological verisimilitude the long digression can be justified by its role as a release; parallels between Hamlet's situation and Krug's – their indecision, the rottenness of the state, their pride, their dragging down others in the tragedy that ensues – can also be adduced as evidence in support of its inclusion.

Seen from a similar perspective, the political statements of the new regime, the language of the constitution, the elaborate justifications of the crassest kind of tyranny and brutality, all these form part of Nabokov's response to the ludicrous posturings of political fanaticism. As in Swift's *Tale of a Tub*, for example, a pseudo-scholarly attention to detail provides 'the logical preparation for the embodied monstrosity' being satirized. Again in the same tradition, minutely detailed accounts of Paduk – he is featured sometimes as a dressmaker's dummy, sometimes as one of the Valkyrie, and finally as dissolving transparency – suggest a significance only to abolish it: 'the precision and pointedness of the description serves simply to give heightening to gross absurdity'.[8]

The difference between the learned wit of the eighteenth century and Nabokov's version of it is that, unlike the academicians, the figures who are the objects his specifically political satire have tended to have the last word, have continued to impose their cruelty no matter how savagely writers make fun of them. Nabokov is, as always, quick to point out the links between pseudo-rational arguments, a general intellectual shoddiness, and political tyranny. Krug is asked to endorse the regime by signing on behalf of his colleagues a document which reads in part:

> We are happy and proud to march with the masses. Blind matter regains the use of its eyes and knocks off the rosy spectacles which used to adorn the long nose of so-called Thought. Whatever I have thought and written in the past, one thing is clear to me now: no matter to whom they belong, two pairs of eyes looking at a boot see the same boot since it is identically reflected in both; and further, that the larynx is the seat of thought so that the working of the mind is a kind of gargling. (150)

Even Chernyshevsky's metaphysical materialism never became quite as addled as this. But for a Paduk, or a Lenin, of course, the contempt of intellectuals is of no great moment, and they with their instruments of torture are confident that will win in the end. Krug is mistaken not to take them seriously, as the novel makes clear, but the conclusion invites us to ponder a set of values that is, for Nabokov, more important than mere survival.

When the end comes, for Krug's beloved son David, for Krug himself, for the regime, for the reader, the formal apparatus of the novel becomes more and more intrusive. How to describe the murder of a child, the impotent frustration of the father and his ultimate madness, the deaths of a group of innocent academics by firing squad? The answer is to make the farce more riotous than ever, and at the same time to impress upon the reader the arbitrariness of the narrative choices being made. Different versions of the same scene are offered; supposed human beings are revealed to be mannequins; levels of reality are conflated; sequences of events are ostentatiously interrupted by the narrator himself. Krug watches a group of criminal psychopaths torture and murder his son as part of their therapy, and thus Nabokov succeeds in representing the ultimate horror while simultaneously satirizing Freudian psychology, which, because of its 'anti-individualism', he (rather unconvincingly) links with Marxist communism.

At this point a great deal depends upon the assumptions one brings to the text itself. Few will be troubled these days by the sudden foregrounding of the text as text. The criticism of many postmodernist writers, including Nabokov, is full of breathless accounts of the vertigo induced by such shifts, but this particular fictional device has lost most of its power to shock, and the credulous, naïve reader who grimly assumes that language gives unmediated access to an independent reality – this creature only continues to exist because he serves as a erstwhile straight man for the critics themselves. But other, more complex assumptions are endorsed or challenged by the text, depending on one's point of view. For those still content with the notion of the author as creator, source, first cause of the text, the conclusion announces the same kind of quiet decency that is offered as an alternative to the cruelty that runs riot in so many of the novels. As Krug is about to be killed, the figure of the author gets up 'from among the chaos of written and rewritten pages' (240) in his quiet study to investigate a moth clinging to the screen of his window. Throughout the text Krug has had a sense of this other order of reality, and after being informed by the author that he is a fictional character, he goes mad. The narrator admits: 'I knew that the immortality I had conferred on the poor fellow was a slippery sophism, a play upon words' (241), which presumably means: Human life does not present its victims with these options, but the world I endorse, where selves can be painlessly created and uncreated, exemplifies the values of sympathetic imagination, the tenderness and curiosity inextricably bound up with the act of uninhibited literary creation, which Western democratic freedoms make possible.

An alternative view which *Bend Sinister* also invites us to consider would treat the cacophony of competing discourses and modes – satire, parody, philosophical treatise, political documents, literary criticism – and the arbitrariness of the ending, as the means by which the novel enacts its own undoing. According to this view, 'Writing a story, discovering a form', becomes for Nabokov 'paradigmatic of the epistemological difficulties' which beset him, his created philosopher, and anyone who attempts to construct a moral order, for that order 'is condemned to be as precarious and provisional as the act of writing itself'.[9] Just as Krug's story revolves around the difficulties he encounters when he insists upon the existence of a moral order independent of the grotesque machinations of the police state that persecutes him, so too does the novel exemplify the difficulties of the writer to embody any sort of reality in the light of twentieth-century history and its horrors. According to this view, the authorial intrusion at the end becomes a kind of sop to bourgeois sentimentality, with no more authority or solace to offer than the hopelessly conventional epilogues in nineteenth-century triple-deckers. Those who insist on the clear moral line of a novel like *Bend Sinister,* a line eloquently reiterated by Nabokov himself in the novel's Introduction, will be impatient with such anti-essentialist readings. But the recuperation of the novel along such lines cannot be peremptorily dismissed. If form and content are indivisible, as Nabokov liked to insist, then one is obliged to acknowledge that the radical innovations of the former sit uneasily alongside the conventional and the prosaic recommendations in the latter.

In the next chapter, we shall encounter similar questions about innovative form and its effect on the reader's reception of the author's moral recommendations. The novels examined in the last two chapters, the studies of the obsessed protagonist and the experiments with the genre itself, provided the basis for the writing of Nabokov's first indisputable masterpiece, *Lolita.*

5

The Morality of the
Aesthete: *Lolita*

The one thing that everyone knows about Nabokov is that he wrote *Lolita*, the book that tells the story of a middle-aged man's lust for a twelve-year-old girl. It began life as a *succès de scandale*, but the novel's popularity with successive generations of readers proves that it satisfies more than prurient interest. Since it was published in 1955, devotees of American fiction have read, in Updike, Roth, Mailer, Burroughs, and Terry Southern, descriptions of sexual encounters more energetic and rococo than anything in *Lolita*, yet it retains its power to shock and surprise. In this chapter, I shall try to explain its enduring appeal, discuss some of the moral and aesthetic issues it raises, and account for its status as one of Nabokov's most important novels.

The first thing we learn from Dr John Ray, Jr, who has written the preface to *Lolita*, is that Humbert Humbert, the articulate, cruel, erudite, intensely self-conscious character who narrates the story has given his manuscript a title, actually two titles, *Lolita, or The Confessions of a White Widowed Male*. These neatly summarize the novel's two subjects: the young girl whose existence has given order and purpose to a twisted life, and the pseudo-scientific, vaguely jocular, literary *tour de force* which is the novel itself. 'Confessions' also inscribes the work in a genre with a long and distinguished history in Western literature. Humbert is aware of the connections with, for example, Rousseau's *Confessions* (he is something of an expert on French literature and will subsequently refer to himself as 'Jean-Jacques Humbert'), and the allusion suggests, as do so many of the myriad references to literature in the novel, a specific parallel. Perhaps the most famous incident in the *Confessions* involves Rousseau's theft of a ribbon while staying in the house of Mme Vercellis, a crime which he blames on an innocent maid who is then severely punished for it. Rousseau seems to revel in the self-condemnation that the recounting of such an incident involves, and at the same time he manages to exculpate himself in a curious way: 'Wicked intent was never further from me than at that crucial moment; and when I accused the unhappy girl, it is contradictory, but it is true, that my affection for her was the cause of what I did'.[1] Before Humbert's confessions are over, the reader will have to make sense of a plethora of similarly tortuous self-justifications, which seek to explain how another 'innocent maid' is blamed and punished because she happens to be the chosen object of male affection. In the process the propounder of these self-justifications will bare his soul much as Rousseau does. And not only his soul. The English philosopher David Hume said of his articulate, cruel, erudite, and intensely self-conscious friend Rousseau: 'He has only *felt* during the whole course of his life, and in this respect his sensibility rises to a pitch beyond what I have seen any example of'.[2] Humbert repeatedly justifies his actions by pleading the extenuating circumstances of being saddled with a similar sensibility. To what extent such a highly-wrought temperament can explain or justify a man's life is one of *Lolita*'s main subjects.

The name of the book's principal female character is the main topic of the first chapter, a chapter that admirably prepares us for the exercise in lyricism and linguistic extravagance to follow. It begins: 'Lolita, light of my life, fire of my loins. My sin, my soul. Lo-lee-ta: the tip of the tongue taking a trip of three steps down the palate to tap, at three, on the teeth. Lo. Lee. Ta' (11). Such an introduction suggests Humbert's dual obsession, the girl and the language that must now serve as a stand-in for her. All the liquid alliteration creates a sense of mobility, of changeableness, yet the possessive pronouns hold the object of desire firmly in place. '[L]ight of my life' means guiding light, but 'life' is also Humbert's synonym for his penis, so the first phrase is actually synonymous with the second, 'fire of my loins'. What he does here to the name he chooses for Dolores Haze, he will do to the person it signifies: to love something for him is to dream of loving it even more by loving it in pieces, by becoming intimately acquainted with all its details. Hence the subsequent references to Humbert's poring over every detail of Lolita's pubescent body: 'My only grudge against nature,' he says at one point, 'was that I could not turn my Lolita inside out and apply voracious lips to her young matrix, her unknown heart, her nacreous liver, the sea-grapes of her lungs, her comely twin kidneys' (167).[3] The mix of goofy comedy, weirdly inappropriate specificity, startling metaphors, and splendid excess exposes the conventionality of the lover's orthodox discourse and offers a bizarre yet curiously compelling substitute for it.

The other topic of Chapter One is the fate theme, which we see in one guise or another in every Nabokov novel, figured variously a coincidence (*Mary*), parodic imitation of hackneyed plots (*King, Queen, Knave*), the pattern of a chess game superimposed on a life (*The Defense*), and so on. In *Lolita*, Humbert will justify much that happens to him as the machinations of one 'McFate', the force that arranges circumstances so that 'in a certain magic and fateful way' (16), his love for Lolita began with a childhood love for Annabel, the young girl to whom he was intensely attracted as a pubescent youth himself. Such 'inevitabilities' function in one sense as blatant rationalizations, of course, but they also suggest Humbert's need to turn his own life into a work of art, with all that that implies about its orderly structure, its gradually unfolding plot, its ultimate significance.

Before Lolita actually appears in the novel, Nabokov's task is to characterize his hero, and this he does in three essential ways: recounting his rather tawdry sexual conquests as a young man in Europe, emphasizing his perversity and cruelty, and drawing our attention to the linguistic means by which Humbert's history presents itself, not as the gloomy case study which Dr Ray's Foreword has prepared us for, but as raucous, irreverent comedy. Reading of Humbert's affairs with prostitutes, his casual brutality to his first wife, his murderous jealousy, one is left with an impression of moral turpitude certainly, but because his moral qualities are mediated through dazzling verbal pyrotechnics, absurd mockery, maniacal scepticism, and sly, self-deprecating humour, one is often too busy laughing to condemn. (Only in the critical responses articulated afterwards do we feel that the earnest pose must be struck, the comedy ignored.)

The events of the next fifteen chapters take place in the typical middle American town in which Humbert discovers Lolita, and Nabokov's task in them is threefold as well: one, describe the foreign country in which Humbert finds himself; two, anatomize and particularize the desire for young girls that is the obsession driving this particular plot; three, create the character Lolita, seen through the shimmer of this desire, as an individual in her own right. The section makes clear that Humbert's perversion is just the most glaring example of a violation of cultural codes that conspire to make him feel like an outsider, and to make him judge that culture harshly as a result. He assumes, for example, that houses decorated with paintings that a cultured European would dismiss as clichés must contain lives which are clichés as well. Consider, for example, part of his introductory description of Lolita's mother, Charlotte Haze:

> She was, obviously, one of those women whose polished words may reflect a book club or bridge club, or any other deadly conventionality, but never her soul; women who are completely devoid of humor; women utterly indifferent at heart to the dozen or so possible subjects of a parlor conversation, but very particular about the rules of such conversations, through the sunny cellophane of which not very appetizing frustrations can be readily distinguished. (39)

That is, she is a typical middle-class woman whose superficiality is an index of her inhumanity, and convention and propriety tyrannize her as they have tyrannized America since the Pilgrim Fathers laid down their rules for the conduct of the community. Humbert in this guise is just one of a long line of European observers – de Tocqueville, Dickens, Arnold, Wilde, D. H. Lawrence – who have noted the slavish conformity that lies paradoxically at the heart of this land founded to build a new freedom.

Of course, one could argue that Humbert's European-style worldly wisdom represents only a veneer disguising the rottenness of a corrupt culture, and that his aesthetic and sexual preferences must be taken as part of a package. Just as the reader must entertain many predictive sequences in the course of reading the novel – Humbert will/will not consummate his passion. Lolita will/will not escape. The law will/will never catch up with this fancy child molester, etc. – so too must a variety of judgements, based on a number of different and even contradictory principles, be considered in the light of successive events. We shall return to this subject, but suffice it to say for now that in these early chapters Humbert's extraordinary verbal energy and rhetorical resources tend to sweep all before them. Again, it is only in retrospect that one asks about the implications of his mocking of middle-class values and his championing of a radical aestheticism as an alternative for an élite.

Nabokov's problem with anatomizing Humbert's desire is to observe decorum without sacrificing lucidity or explicitness entirely. The former is required not only to satisfy readers in America in the 1950s, but because of Nabokov's own very conservative strictures against sexual explicitness in literature. (Despite his enormous admiration for Joyce's work, Nabokov repeatedly commented on the regrettable, unnecessary, off-putting obscenities in *Ulysses*, and Lawrence he dismissed as a pornographer.) The latter is required because leaving the object of Humbert's desire vague will produce the sort of women's magazine romantic slush that the novel itself parodies and denounces. Since Humbert's prose tends towards the purple in any case, this is a genuine risk:

> With these two problems in mind, consider the following example: Only in the tritest of terms can I describe Lo's features: I might say her hair is auburn, and her lips as red as licked red candy, the lower one prettily plump – oh, that I were a lady writer who could have her pose naked in a naked light! But instead I am lanky, big-boned, woolly-chested Humbert Humbert, with thick black eyebrows and a queer accent and a cesspoolful of rotting monsters behind his slow boyish smile. And neither is she the fragile child of a feminine novel. What drives me insane is the twofold nature of this nymphet – of every nymphet, perhaps; this mixture in my Lolita of tender dreamy childishness with a kind of eerie vulgarity, stemming from the snub-nosed cuteness of ads and magazine pictures, from the blurry pinkness of adolescent maidservants in the Old Country (smelling of crushed daisies and sweat); and very young harlots disguised as children in provincial brothels; and then again, all this gets mixed up with the exquisite stainless tenderness seeping through the musk and the mud, through the dirt and the death, oh God, oh God. (46)

Humbert's remark runs the gamut of tones and styles: there is his parody of the 'lady writer', his semi-facetious self-characterization pitched in the language of such a writer as he imagines her, his fascination with the erotic potential of the images of popular culture, and his insistence on the presence of some feeling so powerful, so important, that its intensities somehow justify all the horrors it occasions. Humbert's remarks introduce a tendentious hierarchy of literary forms, in which women's fiction figures far below the (male) novel: in the one, lusty clichés; in the other, something more sharply observed, more accurately and imaginatively conveyed, more faithful. His comments also implicate the culture in the creation of these young girls, linking their vulgarity with advertising, and inviting us to take seriously the proposition that advanced capitalism is in part responsible for his predicament. Again, what disorients us as readers, is that Humbert's critique hits home. Having declared war on tradition, on ideology, on the stability of reality itself in order to make people consume more, capitalism actively works at creating the sort of ethical vacuum into which the Humberts of the world and their casuistical defences naturally rush. As Gerald Graff has argued, 'The essence of capitalistic reality is its unreality, its malleable, ephemeral quality, which provides little in the way of a resisting medium against which personal identity can be formed.'[4] The passage also draws attention to just how often Humbert construes reality as a collection of images taken from weirdly disparate contexts to compose the strange entity which is his world. And, finally, the insertion of phrases like 'diary resumed' and 'Oh God' indicate that Humbert's 'Confessions' are, like Rousseau's, not a spontaneous outpouring of emotion, but a carefully crafted, multilevelled text, requiring multilevelled responses. The very words of this diary, Humbert tells us, are themselves reconstructed from memory, as is the whole account, and the writer's occasional, present-tense jail-cell interpolations on what he is doing adds another dimension as well. What he conveys as involuntary spiritual outburst *à la* Hopkins ('That night of now done darkness I wretch lay wrestling with [my God!] my God') is already rhetoric, part of a dying fall arranged to make the sentence come out correctly.

In the Afterword to *Lolita* Nabokov takes on the question of explicitness, and responds to the accusations of obscenity and pornography levelled at the book on its publication. Since Nabokov's whole approach to the issue involves certain unstated assumptions, let me pause here to make some important distinctions. When Nabokov wrote *Lolita* there were many novels created with the specific purpose of arousing sexual desire, and there is, of course, no *a priori* reason why novels should not perform such a function. At the time *Lolita* was published, John Cleland's *Fanny Hill* was perhaps the most famous example of such a novel. It tends towards the euphemistic, its eroticism being a blend of breathy paeans to oversized organs, yards of white linen and co-operative lingerie, gentle initiations of willing virgins, that kind of thing. A related category works at achieving the same effect but favours a different lexical register altogether. Here four-letter words, stock adjectives, rapturous accounts of quaint gymnastics and quasi-mystical orgasms predominate. In this category the best known work in the 1950s was

Henry Miller's *Tropic of Cancer*, a novel that looks rather tawdry in retrospect, and, at the end of the decade as the result of an important obscenity trial, *Lady Chatterley's Lover*, a heavily didactic lay sermon on lower-class lustiness and the rottenness of the English aristocracy. Contemporary writers tend to imitate these essential types, and of course there is a great deal of parody involved in such imitations, although often the distinction between mimic and model is not always as clear as it might be (see Terry Southern's *Blue Movie*, for example). The third category includes books that are not about sex in any exclusive sense, that are erotic for what they do not say, that none the less mightily offended public morality at the time of publication, and subsequently became literary classics: *Madame Bovary, Anna Karenina, Tess of the d'Urbervilles*.

In Nabokov's account of pornography he implies that he is amused and unoffended by books in category one, mocks with consummate scorn those in category two, and insists that his novel belongs with those in the third group. His incredulity at the initial reactions to *Lolita* now seems a trifle disingenuous – given its subject matter, how could people *not* have been shocked? – but his defence of his novel features his polemical skills at their most impressive. First he characterizes the novels which he feels many readers hoped *Lolita* would imitate:

> action has to be limited to the copulation of clichés. Style, structure, imagery should never distract the reader from his tepid lust. The novel must consist of an alternation of sexual scenes. The passages in between must be reduced to sutures of sense, logical bridges of the simplest design, brief expositions and explanations, which the reader will probably skip but must know they exist in order not to feel cheated . . . Moreover, the sexual scenes in the book must follow a crescendo line, with new variations, new combinations, new sexes, and a steady increase in the number of participants (in a Sade play they call the gardener in) . . .

He goes on to make the interesting claim that *Lolita* is 'sensuous' but not 'sensual' by invoking magazines like *Playboy* as an analogy: 'I can only admire but cannot emulate the accuracy of judgment of those who pose the fair young mammals photographed in magazines where the general neckline is just low enough to provoke a past master's chuckle and just high enough not to make a post master frown' (316). The casual brilliance of the wordplay here should not distract us from the important point being made. Clearly what Nabokov admires about *Playboy* is the wholesomeness of the centrefolds, a product of the soft focus, air brushed, un-raunchy look that Hugh Hefner used to make pictures of bare breasts acceptable in middle-American homes in the late 1950s. *Playboy* consolidated its middlebrow appeal by publishing the work of eminent writers including Nabokov. Still, a vague sense of the risqué remained, only to return with a vengeance as the necklines Nabokov speaks about lowered, post masters looked away, and Hefner's magazine found itself in an explicitness battle with glossy magazines like *Penthouse*. In the years when Nabokov perused it *Playboy* was a much less sleazy affair. He wrote to Hefner in 1967 indicating how much he enjoyed the magazine, and noted that '*Playboy* can always be depended upon to provide brilliant surprises'.[5]

Presumably he set out to do something other than satisfy the readers of such magazines because his character is more than a young mammal, because in his view *Lolita* is a book that belongs in category three rather than category one; that is, its sexual encounters are only incidental. At the level of language the point is well taken. Occasional phrases like 'I gave her to hold in her awkward fist the scepter of my passion' (17), 'a little pubic floss glistened on its plump hillock' (127), or 'Her brown rose tasted of blood' (242) convey as much about Humbert's battles with the language as they do about his grapples with Annabel and Lolita, and even these renderings must have seemed tame to readers first encountering the novel in the Olympia Press edition, more used to titles like 'Debby's Bidet' or 'Tender Thighs'. (It should be added that the Olympia Press also published writers like Genet and Beckett.) Pornography requires willing participants, or failing that, the constraints imposed upon them (chains, handcuffs) must themselves be represented and received as erotic. After the scene in which she and Humbert first have intercourse, Lolita never initiates anything because she is motivated by sexual desire, intense or tepid. And on the whole the erotic power of the sexual scenes in the book is pretty cerebral stuff. The novel that began life as a scandal, and gave nouns like 'nymphet' and 'Lolita' to the language, could never really be anything other than a candidate for the great literature category.

The presentation of Lolita as an individual twelve-year-old, a pre-teen in post-war America, is Nabokov's third task in this first section. The text provides an array of lavish physical descriptions, but these are all Lolita as seen from the outside, Lolita as the object of a desire that consumes its objects, the young girl who has 'individualised the writer's ancient lust' (47), as Humbert puts it. As a coda to a famous masturbation scene in which he uses an unwitting Lolita to reach covert orgasm, Humbert refers to the problem when he notes: 'What I had madly possessed was not she, but my own creation, another, fanciful Lolita – perhaps, more real than Lolita; overlapping, encasing her; floating between me and her, and having no will, no consciousness – indeed, no life of her own' (64). This shows once again how the ethical problems raised in the text are linked to the narrative ones: Humbert attempts to engage our sympathy by assuring us that no real person has been defiled, but if he convinces us of this Nabokov threatens to flatten out his title character, by making her entirely Humbert's creation. And his voice dominates to such an extent that it in effect does threaten to exclude all others, or to reduce them to mere epiphenomena summoned to life from time to time.

In fact, throughout the novel Nabokov has taken pains to indicate that Lolita is more aware even at this early stage than Humbert lets on, and we do hear her voice at times. Snippets of reported speech give evidence of Nabokov's sharp ear (he took notes on buses so that he could reproduce American slang accurately), and he uses them to give us such marvellously revealing fragments as this response to a question about the 'nymphet' that Humbert was tracking when he came to Ramsdale: '"The McCoo girl? Ginny McCoo? Oh, she's a fright. And mean. And lame. Nearly died of polio"' (43). Nabokov's 'little girl', as he liked to refer to her in interviews, comes alive in the novel because she remains an unsentimentalized victim. Then there is Lolita's precocious sexuality. Freud shocked a whole generation by telling it that young children were not sexually innocent but polymorphously perverse; Nabokov was to do the same thing for American parents in the 1950s by suggesting that barely pubescent girls could be sexually active, that adolescence was not an age of innocence either. (The country had been sensitized to questions regarding female sexuality by the publication of Alfred C. Kinsey's *Sexual Behavior in the Human Female* in 1953. 'He is hurling the insult of the century against our mothers, wives, daughters and sisters, under the pretext of making a great contribution to scientific research',[6] intoned one congressman, and many deplored the degradation of American life if what Kinsey said about women's attitudes to sex was true. It is curious to note that Kinsey became interested in human sexuality almost by accident. He began his career as a gifted entomologist whose chief interest was wasps, and published definitive taxonomies of some species. Thus the two authors who did so much to outrage conventional mores in America in the 1950s were both mild-mannered family men with a scientific bent and an interest in specific details.)

It is fitting that Nabokov's most assiduous plotter should appear in his most carefully plotted novel. Having set the scene and introduced all his characters, dangled apparent dream fulfilment in front of his hero, Nabokov's task in the rest of the book is to introduce a series of obstacles to that fulfilment. The first appears naturally enough in the form of Charlotte Haze, who, uninterested in and jealous of her daughter, sends Lolita off to camp for the summer. Humbert's 'McFate' has acted cruelly and unexpectedly indeed. And this precipitates the first of a number of crises in the novel, moments of hesitation, cruces for those keeping track of predictive sequences, points in Humbert's career at which he makes fateful decisions that will crucially determine the course his life will take.

At each of these moments he invokes in an allusion, an imitation, or a parody, the works of Dostoevsky, the novelist who looms so importantly over *Lolita* and over Nabokov's whole career. Why Dostoevsky at these particular moments? Precisely because for so many of Dostoevsky's great characters, for Raskolnikov, Svidrigailov, Ivan Karamazov, and Stavrogin, such moments of hesitation are moments that reveal the very locus of the self, moments at which it asserts itself in a pause as it were. Ceasing to indulge in their characteristically intense and incessant introspection, at these crucial junctures they demonstrate something that exists apart from their endless self-examination and self-inculpation, the bullying and the bravado, the delirium and the desolation. Some adjustment has to be made for the shift from Dostoevskian grandeur to Nabokovian *mesquinerie*, and parody tends to 'double the discourse' as it does in *Despair*, but the links are clear.[7]

The first great 'hesitation' scene occurs when Humbert is suddenly presented with the chance that fate seems to have snatched from him: Charlotte proposes marriage, i.e., offers Humbert the chance of staying close to the object of his one desire, but only if he can successfully feign another. Here is Humbert's reaction:

> After a while I destroyed the letter and went to my room, and ruminated, and rumpled my hair, and modeled my purple

robe, and moaned through clenched teeth and suddenly –
Suddenly, gentlemen of the jury, I felt a Dostoevskian grin
dawning (through the very grimace that twisted my lips) like
a distant and terrible sun. (72)

The comedy in this passage derives from the parody of Dostoevsky's
excessive emotionalism, since the passage recalls the rhetorical
excesses of Dostoevsky's Underground Man in the famous scene in
which, trying to sort out his feelings for a woman who is interested
in him, he models his bathrobe, groans, grimaces, and generally
carries on like someone in a bad romantic novel. Humbert indicates that he has caught himself here in some Dostoevskian posing,
with all that that implies about ersatz emotive effects, fiendish and
nefarious plots, and ostentatiously announced moral turpitude. So
much for his parody. Yet, like Dostoevsky's great novels, *Lolita* is an
analysis of the gap between motive and action, the burden of the
abstract will, the problems involved in any sort of voluntary action
when intense desire is involved, the fallacy implied in assuming that
rebelling against conventional mores necessarily leads to genuine
freedom.

Humbert decides to marry Charlotte, in order to realize his
desire, but in Nabokov's novels fate never gives with one hand
without taking away with the other. Thus Humbert is to learn
within a very short time that Charlotte is sending her daughter
of to boarding school, that his elaborate plans are foiled, that his
sacrifice has been for nothing. This news occasions the second
Dostoevskian hesitation and deliberation:

I had always thought that wringing one's hands was a fictional
gesture – the obscure outcome, perhaps, of some medieval ritual;
but as I took to the woods, for a spell of despair and desperate
meditation, this was the gesture ('look, Lord, at these chains!')
that would have come nearest to the mute expression of my
mood.

The odd combination of a wild hilarity that intrudes upon a
seriously offered anguish marks this as the Dostoevskian mode
again, as does the notion that character defines itself in the gap,
the moment when the hero contemplates his options. Humbert is
about to go for a swim with Charlotte, and the setting is perfect for
'a brisk, bubbling murder' (88), yet he decides, not 'I shall murder
Charlotte Haze', but rather 'Let us see how I react when she and

I find ourselves in the middle of the lake, at the precise moment when, as crime novels tell us, the perfect crime can be committed'. And he can almost do it, but only by dehumanizing her, imagining her as a mermaid, a corpse, a ballerina in a murderous scenario he conjures up. The crisis scene ends with no murder because Humbert's imagination is too grounded in reality. Unlike the old pawnbroker woman in *Crime and Punishment*, who is intensely real to us but a sort of nightmarish fiction to Raskolnikov, Charlotte is too physically there to become a character in someone else's story. For Nabokov, some acts are just intrinsically wrong, and murdering a person is one of them. Humbert has the good fortune to have learned from literature what characters like Raskolnikov must learn from life.

Never content with simply emphasizing the inevitably literary quality of such abstractions as 'the perfect murder', Nabokov adds yet another twist. Charlotte's murder would not, it turns out, have been the perfect crime even if Humbert had been willing to attempt it. Someone was watching them swimming together; life is most devious and unpredictable when we imagine we have it figured out. Soon after, just when Charlotte discovers that Humbert is a fraud and it seems that all his plans are ruined, she is killed in a car accident. Humbert records a range of responses: astonishment at fate's beneficent interference, eagerness to set in motion his plans for Lolita, feigned despair to dupe friends of the family, and some genuine sorrow for Charlotte's death, for the emptiness, the unredeemed quality of her life as he understands it. What marks *Lolita* as different in kind from a novel like *Despair*, is this sort of complex response, the quality of the humanity that makes Humbert more than just an intriguing example of ruthless scepticism, irreverent iconoclasm, and entertaining villainy.

After Humbert takes Lolita from the camp, they put up at a hotel where he drugs her, planning to use the proximity of her body to reach orgasm, and this occasions the third 'hesitation' in our series. As he waits for the drug to take effect, he finds himself involved in an eerie conversation with an interlocutor who apparently possesses intimate knowledge about Humbert's immediate plans, who surprises him with a series of probing questions that put him on the defensive, whose identity seems to shift as the wind and the lighting conditions change, and who talks like Humbert's own bad conscience. Planted throughout the text are clues that Humbert is being shadowed by someone who is also known to and interested in Lolita. We saw how in *Despair* Nabokov plays with the idea of the false double to create a situation in which the hero thinks he is confronted by an image of himself that turns out to be only a projection of his own schizophrenia. In *Lolita* this double figure is another Nabokovian variation on the traditional pattern. But we need to distinguish between two sorts of doubles here. First there is the kind that functions as an embodied distillation of some part of the protagonist's character, a device that is ultimately some version of the dialectical opposition popularized by Freud. In Mary Shelley's 'Transformation', Poe's 'William Wilson', or Stevenson's 'Dr. Jekyll and Mr. Hyde', the self splits into its good and evil counterparts and the battle that results in death permits one or the other to triumph. The other double 'is not so much "deeper in" as "further out"'.[8] Here, again, Dostoevsky serves as an instructive example. The doubles in his novels often act out the secret fantasies and unacknowledged impulses of the principal characters. Svidrigailov in *Crime and Punishment* embodies the existential freedom that Raskolnikov can only dream of, and in *The Brothers Karamazov* Smerdyakov is this sort of double for Ivan, who recognizes his own complicity in Smerdyakov's murder of their father. So too Clare Quilty, Humbert's double, will eventually take Lolita from him and actually gain her love in a way that Humbert never does, but in this scene, his first extended appearance, the suggestive questions and alarming accusations almost frighten Humbert into giving up his plan. Like a Dostoevskian second self, he is a symbol of evil whose actual evil is difficult to pin down, whose appearances are consistently associated with nightmare visions, who has a way of watching and listening that is much more frightening than anything he actually does, and whose final confrontation with the hero of the book is the occasion that results in the undoing of them both.

The seduction scene in *Lolita* is most famous because Lolita does the seducing, or at least she is the one who proposes intercourse and then energetically assists her stupefied companion. Humbert's conclusion is that he is now living in 'a brand new, mad new dream world, where everything was permissible', and again we hear the clear Dostoevskian echo, this time of Ivan Karamazov's conclusion about a world in which the God who exists to forbid things, who constitutes the only possible source of our moral codes, of our very interest in morality, is absent. Ivan's conviction has catastrophic consequences, as does Humbert's. These will be the subject of the second half of *Lolita*, but they are prefigured in what immediately follows the 'lovemaking': 'With the ebb of lust, an ashen sense of awfulness, abetted by the realistic drabness of a gray neuralgic day, crept over me and hummed within my temples' (139) says Humbert. This is a lyrical way of making Freud's point about there being something in the nature of the sexual instinct itself that militates against absolute gratification. Thinking he has opted for a world in which he is free of all constraints, Humbert reminds us in such passages that most people are confined to live out most of their lives in the present, a present that begins to feel particularly constricting as one waits around for lust to 'swell again', as Humbert puts it. While he hesitated, Humbert was still free. Having chosen freedom, he is now in permanent bondage.

It is interesting to contrast this seduction scene with an earlier version of it. In 1939, Nabokov wrote a long story called 'The Enchanter', whose plot resembles *Lolita*'s. The greater physical explicitness of the story makes the whole encounter repulsive in a way that the scene in the novel is not, and shows how Nabokov needs the comedy, the voice that articulates it, and the idea of a complex identity defining itself in the gap between decision and action, if he is to succeed in creating more than just a single effect. The moment of attempted consummation in the story is described this way:

> he also saw how it [his 'rearing nudity'] appeared to her: some monstrosity, some ghastly disease – or else she already knew, or it was all of that together. She was looking and screaming, but the enchanter did not yet hear her screams; he was deafened by his own horror, kneeling, catching at the folds, snatching at the drawstring, trying to stop it, hide it, snapping with his oblique spasm, as senseless as pounding in place of music, senselessly discharging molten wax, too late to stop it or conceal it.[9]

This shows how unerringly Nabokov seized on the defects of the early work and eliminated them. This account implies that there is no pleasure in the act and introduces some stern moralizing in the least appropriate place. The result is curiously old-fashioned, one of those nineteenth-century 'falls' in which the participants seem to have enjoyed no pleasure whatever. The enchanter rushes out after his wild orgasm to throw himself under a handy truck; that is, he shares the stern revulsion for his own desires that Nabokov wants readers to feel for his character's debauchery.[10] Humbert forswears such descriptions altogether, adding only a retrospective comment about how he might have represented the moment of consummation in a mural:

There would have been an arbor in flame-flower. There would have been nature studies – a tiger pursuing a bird of paradise, a choking snake sheathing whole the flayed trunk of a shoat. . . . There would have been a fire opal dissolving within a ripple-ringed pool, a last throb, a last dab of color, stinging red, smarting pink, a sigh, a wincing child. (136–37)

The passage is a good example of how less is more, how delaying the horror makes it more powerful, more verisimilar, and less melodramatic.

'Satire is a lesson, parody is a game',[11] said Nabokov in one interview, distinguishing his novels from those of didactic writers, and identifying himself as a subtle player of elaborate games in a world where most novels are written by the pretentious and solemn purveyors of moral lessons. But the two modes are not as distinct as his remark implies. The parodist who exposes folly and vice to ridicule is at least a part-time satirist, whether his main purpose is teaching a moral lesson or not, and the second half of *Lolita* involves Nabokov in satirizing those aspects of America he finds ridiculous. Some of this satire merely develops at greater length the critique of middle-class philistinism and consumerism found in Part One. But Nabokov has a new interest in this general area, and it is linked to the scene just examined. Seeking to account for the 'depravity' of his nymphet, Humbert cites 'modern co-education' as one of the principal causes. (Nabokov speaks disparagingly of progressive education in a number of interviews and in the Preface to *Invitation*).

In Part Two, having travelled the length and breadth of America and surveyed its mores by describing the motel culture and the tourist attractions, Humbert settles in a small New England town and sends Lolita to school. This encounter with American education fills a large pause in the novel while the forces conspiring to wrest Lolita from her 'protector' conspire and wait. Nabokov represents the progressive wing of the educational establishment in the figure of Miss Pratt, Lolita's Headmistress at Beardsley School, who describes her pedagogical philosophy this way:

'while adopting certain teaching techniques, we are more interested in communication than in composition. That is, with due respect to Shakespeare and others, we want our girls to *communicate* freely with the live world around them rather than plunge into musty old books. . . the position of a star is important, but

the most practical spot for an icebox in the kitchen may be even
more important to the budding housewife'. (179–80)

Miss Pratt's non-curriculum threatens the humanistic education
Humbert so vaguely believes in, but she threatens him as well. Like
so many foolish people mocked in *Lolita*, she is someone whose
earnest stupidity is in one sense preferable to all of Humbert's
cunning intelligence.

Bakhtin's remarks on the way in which the fool 'makes strange'
the world of social convention by refusing to understand it are
apposite here, for they shed light on the exact nature of the confrontation between Lolita's two delinquent educators. He writes:

> Stupidity in the novel is always polemical: it interacts dialogically
> with an intelligence (a lofty pseudo-intelligence) with which it
> polemicizes and whose masks it tears away. . . . Stupidity in the
> novel is always implicated in language, in the word: at its heart
> always lies a polemical failure to understand someone else's dis-
> course, someone else's pathos-charged lie that has appropriated
> the world and aspires to conceptualize it, a polemical failure
> to understand generally accepted, canonized, inveterately false
> languages with their lofty labels for things and events.[12]

Although Bakhtin has in mind here characters like Sancho Panza
in *Don Quixote*, who insists on seeing windmills where his master's
overwrought imagination projects monsters, or Fabrice in *La Char-
treuse de Parme*, who can discern only chaos at Waterloo where the
generals perceive battle lines unveiling themselves in neat and intricate order, the words are relevant to this scene in *Lolita* as well. For
Miss Pratt is 'stupid' in two senses. Her idea of education is idiotic
(and hopelessly conservative as well, since all she aspires to do for
her girls is to make them good housewives), but simply by offering
an alternative discourse, she reminds the reader that Humbert
brings a 'lofty pseudo-intelligence' to the task of being a parent,
and that his 'pathos-charged lie', anyone's lie, has the power to
assert itself in a moral vacuum. Steeping oneself in Western culture
à la Humbert does not necessarily make one a better person; Miss
Pratt's 'stupidity' is a bad alternative but a decent one. (One
notes in passing that Beardsley's minimalist pragmatic approach
to learning functions at the expense of scientific education as well
as the Humanities, and here Nabokov has accurately depicted the
system in place when *Lolita* was written. America in the early 1950s

is the country in which science students were still being taught that
God made the flowers out of sunshine. Only when the Soviet Union
orbited the first satellite in 1957 did the science curriculum begin
to change.)

After one more cross-country journey, Lolita escapes, and
Nabokov telescopes time so that the three years she is missing pass
in a couple of chapters. When she finally writes asking for money,
Humbert tracks her down and sees her for the last time. In this
crucial scene three things are revealed, and the novel features the
last great 'hesitation' before the confrontation between Humbert
and Quilty and the final curtain.

First, Humbert learns from Lolita the name of his rival, but he
does not give the name to the reader. At this point, only the most
attentive will realize, by piecing together all the clues, that Clare
Quilty is responsible for 'saving' her from Humbert. Thus the
moment everything becomes clear for the hero it usually does not
for the first-time reader, which underlines the gap between her task
as part-time sleuth and his obsession with finding his rival. For him,
the great revelation is everything, and he recounts it, revealingly, in
the language of male arousal and orgasm with which he identifies
aesthetic response to perceived pattern:

> everything fell into order, into the pattern of branches that I
> have woven throughout this memoir with the express purpose
> of having the ripe fruit fall at the right moment; yes, with the
> express and perverse purpose of rendering – she was talking but
> I sat melting in my golden peace – of rendering that golden and
> monstrous peace through the satisfaction of logical recognition.
> (274)[13]

The second thing not revealed stems from Lolita's refusal to
describe in detail what she did with Quilty and his friends. What
is left unspecified here establishes her as a moral entity in her
own right, capable of making choices, ludicrously 'in love' with
a hopeless degenerate, but faithful to her decent husband, the
baby she is to have by him, and her future. Humbert's feeling
for her, if he still feels it now that she is too old to be a mythical
creature, must be more than an adoration lavished on his own
creation.

Which leads us to the third non-revelation in this last scene,
what Humbert tells the reader but not Lolita, his confession of
love:

> there she was with her ruined looks and her adult, rope-veined
> hands and her goose-flesh white arms, and her shallow ears, and
> her unkempt armpits, there she was (my Lolita!), hopelessly
> worn at seventeen, with that baby, dreaming already in her of
> becoming a big shot and retiring around 2020 A.D. – and I looked
> and looked at her, and knew as clearly as I know I am to die, that
> I loved her more than anything I had ever seen or imagined on
> earth, or hoped for anywhere else. (279)

Humbert goes on to 'cancel' and 'curse' his 'sterile and selfish vice'
in the same lexical register, with the same kind of lyrical intensity.
With a writer as tricky and parodic as Nabokov, the tendency has
understandably been to read warily even in such places, and one
critic has made an ingenious case for the proposition that Humbert
invents the entire last episode, that he never meets with Lolita at
all, this despite Nabokov's own comments about the ending as
an entirely legitimate and significant part of the whole.[14] The
important irony in such passages involves the reader's recognition
that Humbert's love is not betrayed by his language but limited
by his very situation, that his declaration is written not spoken,
destined for the only 'auditors' who are capable of understanding
what it means. Like almost all of Nabokov's protagonists, Humbert
is finally incapable of the love that has fascinated novelists for
more than three centuries, and not just because the object of it
is so young. Love provides him with no access to Lolita's inner
reality, not only because she refuses him access but also because
his very nature would prevent him from taking advantage of such
an opportunity. When one thinks of the great love stories of the
last century, *Wuthering Heights, Anna Karenina,* or of this one,
*Women in Love, À la recherche du temps perdu, Farewell to Arms, The
French Lieutenant's Woman, Love in the Time of Cholera,* one is struck
by how limited or problematic or ambiguous or unconventional
the male's commitment to the central relationship is in each of
these novels, how only intermittently can he be seen as engaged
with love as a process, what D. H. Lawrence calls the 'long event of
perpetual change, in which a man and a woman mutually build up
their souls and make themselves whole'.[15] And if one admits this to
be the case with such novels, then however the formulation of this
'limitation' is finally articulated, it will surely be *a fortiori* true of a
novel like *Lolita.* For it is finally a moving account of a magnificent
obsession that explores the boundaries of one consciousness, one
world, not the interaction of two.

Humbert's last 'hesitation' occurs after he has left Lolita and gone in search of Quilty. Humbert pauses in the middle of an empty town, and having surveyed the detritus of the cheap commercialism that surrounds him, he takes a last look at himself and his love for this girl whom he will never see again. He begins by recalling how a Catholic priest was unsuccessful in helping him deduce from his sense of sin 'the existence of a Supreme Being', and continues:

> Alas, I was unable to transcend the simple human fact that whatever spiritual solace I might find, whatever lithophanic eternities might be provided for me, nothing could make my Lolita forget the foul lust I had inflicted upon her. Unless it can be proven to me – to me as I am now, today, with my heart and my beard, and my putrefaction – that in the infinite run it does not matter a jot that a North American girl-child named Dolores Haze had been deprived of her childhood by a maniac, unless this can be proven (and if it can, then life is a joke), I see nothing for the treatment of my misery but the melancholy and very local palliative of articulate art. To quote an old poet:
>
>> The moral sense in mortals is the duty
>> We have to pay on mortal sense of beauty. (284–85)

The Dostoevskian note is, of course, the echo of 'everything is permitted' in Humbert's deliberations ('in the infinite run it does not matter a jot'), a phrase that rings rather hollowly now. For Humbert is wrong in at least one important sense: Lolita has forgotten; it is he who cannot forget, and who cannot find spiritual solace as a result. His crime, which seemed so simple and straightforward at the outset, a matter of swooping up maidens on 'islands of entranced time' and depositing them there when done with them, involved him in enormous complications and occasioned real human suffering. A self-spun moral philosophy cannot supply what he needs because the question 'Why should I not ravish young girls?' has no meaning in the decentred world, devoid of authority, that he has discovered. What he has done to Lolita does matter, but only because it matters to him. He condemns himself because he feels bad, because what he has done has made retelling his story so painful.[16]

But what does art have to do with it? Is there not something tendentious and self-serving about the claim that the moral sense and the aesthetic work together? After all, Humbert's aesthetic sense was eminently well developed before he ever set eyes on

Lolita, and look what happened. So how is it that we must pay a 'duty'? The argument can be paraphrased this way: 'Those as keenly sensitive to beauty as I am [remember the descriptions of Lolita, of American landscapes] know that the principal reason we are so responsive to it is its fluid, changeable quality, its existence in time. And such a sense has, not a moral component exactly, but something that enables us to attach a value to existence, to comprehend its evanescent nature. Lapses from this high standard occur, but the principle is a sound one. Such lapses can be atoned for in part by creating harmony from the chaos one has wrought in everyday life, by revealing its underlying patterns as I have done in this account.' Every reader must decide how successfully Humbert makes his complicated case.

The novel might well have ended there. After all, the loose ends have been tied up, the conclusions drawn. But the confrontation with Quilty remains to be acted out, partly because Nabokov wants to parody the conventional ending of the 'double' story in which evil is confronted and exorcised, partly because his gift for black humour faces a sort of ultimate test here, an on-stage murder, partly because he has to loosen his narrator's hypnotic hold on us by making him more detestable.

In the first part of their encounter Humbert attempts to conduct a mock trial but Quilty refuses to play the role he has been scripted for. 'Now who are you?' he asks at the outset, and the question, like the 'Who's there?' that is the opening line of *Hamlet*, prepares the reader for yet another scene in which the protagonist, in contemplating his own motives and actions, is forced to see himself in a new context. In a scuffle over the gun, Nabokov plays with pronouns ('I rolled over him. We rolled over me. They rolled over him. We rolled over us' [301]) to suggest a blending of identities, but then follows a long monologue in which Quilty reveals just how the two characters are to be distinguished: he is on drugs, he keeps as a 'house pet' a girl with three breasts, he is blackmailing the police chief, he likes pornography and executions . . . in other words, Humbert starts to look like an outraged avenging angel eliminating a vile misfit. And yet, as Nabokov knows perfectly well, evil is not to be quantified in this way; the moral distinction implied by the contrast suggests only a difference in degree. The protracted and outrageous murder that ensues demolishes all the elaborate moral calculus set up by the contrast, and makes readers as eager for Humbert's ultimate demise as they were curious about his attempts at self-justification.

At the end of the novel, as Humbert is about to be arrested, he recalls 'a last mirage of wonder and hopelessness' that he witnessed while searching for Lolita. From a mountain road he surveys a small mining town in a distant valley below. The visual impression, as always lovingly and unforgettably etched by Nabokov, is here superseded by the aural:

> Reader! What I heard was but the melody of children at play, nothing but that, and so limpid was the air that within this vapor of blended voices, majestic and minute, remote and magically near, frank and divinely enigmatic – one could hear now and then, as if released, an almost articulate spurt of vivid laughter, or the crack of a bat, or the clatter of a toy wagon . . . . I stood listening to that musical vibration from my lofty slope, to those flashes of separate cries with a kind of demure murmur for background, and then I knew that the hopelessly poignant thing was not Lolita's absence from my side, but the absence of her voice from that concord. (310)

This is a great conclusion, because it resolves key issues for certain readers, and leaves in suspense all the tensions that so intrigue others. It says that Humbert has robbed Lolita of her childhood; thus he stands condemned, self-condemned. The lyrical evocation reinforces the intensity, and the allusion to a final harmony from which the discordant Humbert is excluded suggests that he remains marginal to the end. The text has also come more or less full circle, back to the days when he listened in on Lolita and her friends at Ramsdale. Those less interested in finality will seize on other aspects of the ending, on the ways in which, whatever his intentions, Humbert undermines his own attempts at imposing closure. Nietzsche's observation that those who despise themselves nevertheless esteem themselves as self-despisers hovers ominously over such passages. According to this view, the voices are 'frankly enigmatic' because they say different things to different people. Humbert's regret for Lolita's loss of her childhood is a threnody for time passing, including the loss of his own childhood, not a confrontation with his guilt. She was hardly a child when she met him, and he took from her, not playtime with friends and their 'toy wagons', but the possibility of normal adult experience. Besides, 'American childhood' has been revealed in the course of his narrative to be something rather different from the innocent play described here: 'the Miranda twins had shared the same bed for years, and Donald Scott . . . had done it with Hazel Smith in his uncle's garage, and Kenneth Knight . . . used to exhibit himself wherever and whenever he had a chance' (138–39) – so runs Lolita's account of her coevals. The passage, seen in this light, represents one more appeal to an illusory Lolita by a deluded Humbert.

The coda of the novel will support such opposed readings as well. In it, Humbert says goodbye to Lolita, who is no longer living when the authorities publish Humbert's book, and promises her an immortality of sorts in the work of art he has created. This is more profound and moving sincerity for many, different in kind from the self-serving and self-regarding effusions that characterize earlier parts of the text. 'I am thinking of aurochs and angels, the secret of durable pigments, prophetic sonnets, the refuge of art,' says Humbert. The aurochs is a species of extinct buffalo, the angel an imaginary creation of religious mystics, yet they live on in accounts that describe them, as do the faces of those memorialized in an artist's 'durable pigments', or the beloved figure in the world's great love poems.

For others, Humbert's threats, contained in the very last lines of the book, to kill by slow torture Lolita's husband if he mistreats her are much more to the point. Sexual jealousy and possessiveness have always been Humbert's subject. According to this view, even when he condemns himself to thirty-five years for rape, he is engaging in a rhetorical flourish only, since his posing as ultimate judge and jury was what got him and Lolita into so much trouble in the first place. In fact, the very life/art antithesis his last words introduce is suspect, since this tidy distinction is precisely the one the novel has worked so hard to subvert. Only notional creatures can find solace in the immortality offered by sonneteers and portrait artists eager for exorbitant commissions, and thus Humbert contents himself in the end by ascribing a hackneyed, bookish reality to the person whose independent reality he has never been able to acknowledge. The plausibility of such different accounts is surely the one of the main reasons the novel continues to be so popular.

The above description of *Lolita* is accurate as far as it goes, but it downplays the novel's self-reflexive qualities, its elaborate games, its interrogation of the status of the novel and of fiction itself. Recent movements in literary criticism have sought to 'undermine the referential status of language', subvert 'received ideas about the text, the context, the author, the reader', undo 'the very

comforts of mastery and consensus that underlie the illusion that
objectivity is situated somewhere outside the self', 'show the text
resolutely refusing to offer any privileged reading', serve as the
antithesis of any mode of reading that subscribes to 'traditional
values and concepts', and to prove that meaning is 'ultimately
indeterminate'.[17] Any critic who attempts to approach texts in
these ways would seem to have found the ideal text in *Lolita*.
Note that the above propositions tend to be descriptive rather
than prescriptive; that is, they explain what all literature does, not
what certain authors should do. But the writers who helped bring
such critical concerns into being were, of course, those who wrote
the books that posed most openly and directly the new questions
about tradition and authority, about referentiality and the nature
of language, the questions that have loomed so importantly for
academic critics in recent years.

Theoretically minded readers would explore at greater length
the ways in which Humbert's narrative unwittingly subverts itself.
For example, by presenting us with a 'father' who is the 'lover'
of his 'daughter', and a 'child' who is denied a childhood, it
makes for an ominous gap or silence at the heart of the book
after Charlotte is killed, the counterpart to the gap left by the
silence about sex itself. Critics concerned about the logocentrism
of Western culture might adduce comments like 'Repeat until
the page is full, printer', in Humbert's ostentatiously 'written'
text, as evidence for his assigning a priority to the written as
opposed to the spoken confession, and a preference for writing
over speech that subverts the traditional position of these two
in Western thought. So too with the culture/nature dichotomy.
When Humbert insists: 'I have but followed nature. I am nature's
faithful hound', he reminds us that *Lolita*'s revision of sexuality
reveals the vacuity of the attempt to divide up experience into
these conventional categories. His argument is in one sense a
case of preposterous special pleading, since for genetic reasons
nature works against incest by natural selection; but the standards
of conduct set by parents and children and the limits of desire are
cultural constructs whose assumptions his story seeks to undercut.
It is true that such criticism can divert attention from material that
is equally relevant. For example, after his comment about nature,
quoted above, Humbert says 'Why then this sense of horror that
I cannot shake off?' As so often in Nabokov, here the subversion
is accompanied by a reversion to traditional morality. Of course,
such pronouncements need have no special status, and one can

easily imagine a critique that reveals them to be simply elaborate parodies of an ideology that requires moralistic tags to conclude its stories. But the point is that an appeal to internal evidence cannot by itself resolve such questions. The values that inform any set of critical criteria may well be contingent, in the sense that they are human creations and not eternal laws; our task is to determine how well such criteria perform the function we have set for them.

Raising such questions about *Lolita* is useful in another sense as well, for they point us in the direction that Nabokov's fiction eventually took. The novels he went on to write both illustrate and interrogate the problematic relations between self and world. In the next chapter we shall look at three of them with a view to analyzing the extent and the significance of their relation to the new ideas about fiction that took hold in America in the 1960s and 1970s.

6

Metafictions:
Pale Fire, Ada, and
Look at the Harlequins!

The novels discussed in this chapter represent a new departure for Nabokov. Whereas in almost all of his earlier work readers can assume certain basic things about the probable people and events represented in the novels, no matter how much the linguistic and narratological games the author plays divert attention from the novel's mimetic function, in late Nabokov the questioning of such conventions becomes more pronounced. The humour and pathos that derive in previous novels from the conflict between the yearning for self-assertion and the need for self-control become less important; the puns, wordplay, allusions, parody, and rapid-fire interlingual jokes become more so. The earthbound character of even his more fantastic work, which provided a centre of gravity for the elaborate aesthetic patterns, changes radically. And the generalized readership Nabokov attracted in novels like *Lolita* and *Pnin* begins to feel lost without some help from academic critics and their special kind of professionalized discourse. For these reasons, many commentaries on Nabokov's late fiction take the form of annotations and explanations, and attempts to show how it illustrates Nabokov's own aesthetic precepts. In what follows I shall try to provide both useful information of this sort and to evaluate some of those precepts themselves. The best justification for reading Nabokov is his idiosyncratic combination of articulate intelligence, rarefied sensitivity and agile imagination. When he lapses from his own high standards, it is no insult to the master to point it out.

In the last thirty years, fiction that interrogates its own status has often been described as 'postmodern' but, like 'romanticism' for an earlier generation, 'postmodernism' has proved an elusive term to pin down. It has been variously defined as a combination of 'apocalyptic despair' and 'visionary celebration', 'the literature of replenishment', a recapitulation of certain modernist concerns, a subversion of certain modernist concerns, 'a stage on the road to the spiritual unification of mankind', 'the cultural logic of late capitalism', 'the simulacrum gloat[ing] over the body of the deceased referent', 'enlightened false consciousness', literature that is 'radically resistant to totalizing interpretation', a game played for its own sake that ostentatiously refuses to interfere with the world, a revival of 'the early romantic vision of a unified world, but experienced this time as a frightening reality', and a paradoxical mix of 'complicity and critique, of reflexivity and historicity, that at once inscribes and subverts the conventions and ideologies of the dominant cultural and social forces of the twentieth-century western world'.[1]

The novels to be considered in this chapter fit some of these definitions better than others, but all these descriptions can help orient readers attempting to understand these diverse texts. Take *Pale Fire*, for example. It is a novel that is built around a poem, 'Pale Fire', written by John Shade, a sort of poor man's Robert Frost whom Nabokov has invented for the purpose, and a Commentary written by one Charles Kinbote. Even its hybrid status invites questions about the meaning of words like 'novel' that are germane to the postmodernist enterprise. But although it contains much that would make it a candidate for any version of this particular 'ism', unlike the fiction of Abish, Beckett, Cortázar, Duras, Eco, Federman, *et al.*, the names that crop up again and again when one thinks about what constitutes a postmodernist text, Nabokov's novel doesn't *feel* as if it was written to illustrate a particular truth about post-anything. It exists apart. So while it is plausible to argue, working one's way through the list of definitions cited above, that *Pale Fire* pits solipsistic despair against visionary celebration, offers new possibilities and combinations for the 'exhausted' genre of the novel, uses its fragmented status to disorient and compel the reader to take an active rôle in the creation of the text, challenges the modernist view of art as the autonomous expression of individual subjectivity, features a weird conflation of identities that might well be taken as the evidence of 'spiritual reunification' at some level, flaunts a disdainful and dilettantish aestheticism which attempts to mask the real reasons for the profound socio-economic upheavals it indirectly chronicles, banishes forever the idea of a real world which language exists to re-create, isolates and examines the false consciousness of characters who entertain naïve assumptions about a world beyond that will somehow redeem the inequities of this one, presents a Chinese-box view of reality and fiction that subverts any attempt to arrive at a comprehensive reading, redefines the novel as an elaborate, multilevelled acrostic, revives the romantic attempt to seal up the split between subject and object, only to depict it as a plunge into a solipsistic nightmare, and uses parody to play in the paradoxical space between espousing and subverting the narratological, cultural and political conventions of America and Europe in the early 1960s – such descriptions only partly prepare the reader for an encounter with the actual text. For one thing, it is much more fun to read than such austere renderings make it sound. To characterize the novel as an oddly moving, madcap romance, supersaturated with dazzling cross-references by a trilingual writer of genius, sounds rather old-fashioned, but comes closer to describing what less theoretically-minded readers are more likely to experience. That having been said, substantial essays could be written on the novel as seen from every one of the above perspectives (and from a dozen others that define the postmodernist enterprise), which should give some sense of what a responsive object Nabokov has provided for our meditations. (Readers are invited to examine *Ada* and *Look at the Harlequins!* from each of the above perspectives as well.)

The other aspect of *Pale Fire*'s construction that makes it particularly relevant for critics today is that the commentary constitutes a truly splendid example of deconstructive reading, a recontextualization of a text into a Commentary. Frustrated by not finding what he wants in the poem, Kinbote, anticipating Jacques Derrida, at times breaks words into phonemes to 'discover' the subject matter he yearns to discuss. His efforts in this regard emphasize how the casual, accidental aspects of any text can be a source for imaginative flights in another, creative sphere. In arranging for his mad hero to proceed as he does, Nabokov anticipates both the methods of post-structuralist critics and their preoccupations, the notion of language as a play of differences, the revealing of self-referential paradox and self-conscious indeterminability, the emphasis on interpretation as misinterpretation, the arbitrariness of the boundaries between 'truth and falsity, sense and nonsense, reason and madness, central and marginal',[2] the conflict between the totalizing requirements of a structure, on the one hand, and the element of play which resists the implied notions of closure in the idea of structure, on the other. Yet *Pale Fire* not only seems to encourage such a reading but also offers an insightful criticism of its fundamental precepts, thus reminding us that, like *Lolita*, this novel resists appropriation by any single set of critical criteria.

In a Preface, the annotator of 'Pale Fire' includes some instructions for reading this strange text, instructions that make his own commentary pre-eminent, but since the poem itself is the *sine qua non* of the whole exercise, it is perhaps the most appropriate starting point. John Shade's 999-line lyric meditation on life and death, written in heroic couplets, divides up into four sections. In the first, the poet begins by reflecting on the complex qualities of the poetic imagination:

> I was the shadow of the waxwing slain
> By the false azure of the windowpane;
> I was the smudge of ashen fluff – and I
> Lived on, flew on, in the reflected sky.
>
> (33)

This is in one sense a Romantic commonplace, Keats's 'negative capability', that protean quality of the poet's imagination that enables him to transcend boundaries and to assume a variety of identities. The lines also tell us that to be fooled by a mere reflection can mean death, that what seems like an opening can actually be a barrier. Yet, paradoxically, the window, the misleading mirror, is no barrier, because the accident it occasions enables the poet to participate vicariously in the life it destroys, and thus the bird flies on in the poet's recreation of it. Shade enjoys the conflation of worlds occasioned by such reflections (in both senses of the word), as, for example, when an illuminated domestic interior is imposed upon the dark world outside. This in turn leads him to muse about reading the world as a text, in the black marks made by a pheasant's feet on the snow, or in any sequence of events that suggests a certain significance. The poet goes on to draw a distinction between a 'vulgar' cynicism which denies all reality to the notion of an afterlife, and his own form of agnosticism which makes each of us windowless monads, unable even to imagine adequately a hereafter, for '*if* prior to life we had/ Been able to imagine life, what mad,/ Impossible, unutterably weird,/ Wonderful nonsense it might have appeared!' (40–41). Like the non-poet, who is oblivious to the wonder of the stars, the mysteries inherent in the startling poetry of galactic immensity, those who take an unimaginative, commonsensical position on any question of spiritual import are wrong from the start. If '*Life is a message scribbled in the dark.*/ Anonymous' (41), then the emphasis must be on the attempt to reconstitute the communicative link implied by this conviction.

The poet muses extensively about death: his teenage daughter committed suicide, and Shade himself has had a number of near-death experiences. According to 'Pale Fire' there are two ways of talking about death: the farcical discussion at 'I.P.H.', the Institute of Preparation for the Hereafter, represents one alternative, with its advice to ghosts and twice-married widowers. This way lies silliness, as does the whole table-rapping, ectoplasmic otherworld in all its crude manifestations. Wallace Stevens muses somewhere about how unutterably vulgar an afterlife would be that did *not* resemble the one we know, and Shade echoes these sentiments when he lists his conditions for everlasting life:

> And I'll turn down eternity unless
> The melancholy and the tenderness
> Of mortal life; the passion and the pain;
> The claret taillight of that dwindling plane
> Off Hesperus; your gesture of dismay
> On running out of cigarettes; the way
> You smile at dogs; the trail of silver slime
> Snails leave or[3] flagstones; this good ink, this rhyme,
> This index card, this slender rubber band
> Which always forms, when dropped, an ampersand,
> Are found in Heaven by the newly dead
> Stored in its strongholds through the years.

(53)

In 'The Art of Literature and Common Sense', Nabokov defines the 'capacity to wonder at trifles' that Shade articulates here as one of 'the highest forms of consciousness', advocates reading both literature and life in this way, and insists that 'it is in this childishly speculative state of mind, so different from commonsense and its

logic, that we know the world to be good'.[4] Critics once sneered at
F. R. Leavis for what they saw as his attempt to arrest the Decline of
the West by close reading. The ethical consequences that Nabokov
associates with the ability to notice trifles are less earnestly phrased
than Leavis's, and he envisions the redemption of individuals rather
than a whole society; but he does believe that those who have the
ability to see life and art in this way (Nabokov mentions 'thousands'
of fellow dreamers in the same essay) in a sense do not have to
worry about immortality, because they have had a glimpse of it
here, in this 'highest form of consciousness'. The intensity of the
good reader's response to these details leaves him in a realm where
the mysteries that have proved so baffling for philosophy and its
general ideas simply drop away, and the feeling itself becomes a
sort of guarantee of aesthetic immortality, and represent as much
of paradise as we can know.

'Pale Fire' makes clear that any truth about such matters will be
of the subjective variety only. When Shade almost dies of a heart
attack, he sees a 'white fountain' in what he takes to be eternity,
and becomes tremendously excited when he learns that another on
the brink of death has seen the same object. Alas, it turns out that
what this woman saw was a *m*ountain, and Shade ruefully concludes:

> Life Everlasting – based on a misprint!
> I mused as I drove homeward: take the hint,
> And stop investigating my abyss?
> But all at once it dawned on me that this
> Was the real point, the contrapuntal theme;
> Just this: not text, but texture; not the dream
> But topsy-turvical coincidence,
> Not flimsy nonsense, but a web of sense.
> Yes! It sufficed that I in life could find
> Some kind of link-and-bobolink, some kind
> Of correlated pattern in the game,
> Plexed artistry, and something of the same
> Pleasure in it as they who played it found.
>
>   (62–63)

On the face of it, this seems somewhat trivial and bathetic after
the elaborate preamble. A recommendation to spend one's time
finding patterns in the game of life, which is played against invisible
forces who, like Thomas Hardy's 'Immortals' but without their

blind indifference, manipulate events and human destinies? Surely this is just a transposed version of the old formalist concentration on surface details with all of its manifest inadequacies? But Shade's argument is informed by the 'trifles noticing' metaphysic described above, and he adds to that the notion that meanings do not inhere in things but in the relations between them. Significantly, he resigns himself at the end of the poem to admitting that such a formula has enabled him to understand only a 'minute part' of his existence; that is, a great deal of work remains to be done. Man's life is, he goes on to note, only 'commentary to abstruse / Unfinished poem' (67). The pattern that has evolved so far leaves him reasonably assured that there is life after death for his daughter, life after art for him, that he will wake up the next day and continue to play his game of worlds. (At least some of this confidence is misplaced: he is about to be killed by a crazed gunman.)

The poststructuralist critics cited earlier on the subject of the postmodernist text would simply push this argument a step further. For them, Nabokov has thematized here the yearning for the transcendental signifier, for that which reveals an unquestionable meaning, an ultimate essence, something that exists beyond our language and conceptual systems. In exposing this notion as a fiction, *Pale Fire* reminds us that there is no origin from which all other meanings flow, just as there is no goal, no teleological view of literature or language or history which would reveal where we are all headed.[5] There is only the infinite complexity of interrelated texts, the relationships that baffle and intrigue and inform and delight us as we move back and forth between the world and our commentaries on it. Of course, for such critics *all* literature performs a similar function, but Nabokov's novel is of particular interest because it both conceptualizes and enacts these precepts.

The poem is left unfinished, trailing away in a description of more details, the setting sun, his wife's shadow seen from a window, a butterfly. The last line, l. 1000, is unwritten, but just as Shade's chief rival Robert Frost recycles a line at the end of his famous 'Stopping by Woods on a Snowy Evening' to give it a new meaning in a new context, so too does Shade borrow 'I was the shadow of the waxwing slain', the first line of his poem, to rhyme with l. 999. Like Frost, he wants to end with the notion of death, but a death that celebrates the vicarious life of the romantic imagination, the immortality that Shade hopes to gain with his 'Pale Fire'.

The rhyming couplet, the autobiographical long poem, the poet's

belief in a personal immortality conferred by the timelessness of art
– in the twentieth century these have all gone the way of the waxwing, but, like it, John Shade's verse survives because of the creative
imagination of someone else. Charles Kinbote, a lunatic who fancies
himself the deposed King of an imaginary country called Zembla,
has provided Shade's work with a Foreword, a Commentary, and
an Index. In the Foreword, he gives us a taste of the very personal
sort of scholarship to which 'Pale Fire' has been subjected, and the
Commentary makes clear that Shade's poem is to serve as a mere
point de départ for the political romance that Kinbote is committed
to telling us. The Index constitutes a complex of cryptic allusion
and hilarious detail that serves as a gloss on the commentator's
eccentricities.

Although a great deal of the humour of what follows derives from
the fact that poem and commentary have nothing to do with each
other, Nabokov has bound the two together with a truly astonishing
number of extraordinarily suggestive cross references. An entire
book has been written to explicate such matters,[6] but part of
the fun is making one's own connections. The whole notion of
turning over to the reader an important part of the creative act
is one that *Pale Fire* takes perfectly seriously. At the same time the
author maintains a kind of general control over the meaning of
the events depicted. For example, he wants readers to know that
Kinbote is crazy, that he is not Charles II of Zembla but V. Botkin,
a member of the Russian Department at the university where Shade
teaches, that the man who accidentally shoots John Shade is not an
assassin come to destroy a deposed European monarch, but a killer
keen to take revenge on the judge who has sent him to prison. All
of this information slowly comes together for readers who want to
get the identities straight. But – and this is the real magic of the
novel – just as one has assigned the proper names and roles to the
appropriate figures, they start to blend once again.

Of any number of examples that could be chosen, consider
Jakob Gradus, Kinbote's supposed assassin. Kinbote repeatedly
denounces those who see him as only a humble actor in a vulgar
tale of botched revenge, thus alerting us to the fact that in one
sense that is all Jack Grey is. At the same time, such claims remind
us that, for Nabokov, the more imaginative reading of a set of events
is always to be preferred in such circumstances. (Remember Shade
on the subject of the galaxies.) Kinbote reports that Gradus begins
his journey to New Wye on Shade's birthday, July 5, but he adds that

the would-be regicide's departure should be synchronized with the moment that Shade actually begins his poem, shortly after midnight on July 2. Gradus arrives at the end of the poem, and his name is the last word to appear in the Commentary as well. So from one perspective Gradus is, not a figment of a maniac's imagination, but someone whose progress is inexorable and whose success in the physical world is certain, an irresistible force, one-way time itself, that thing bound up with the beginning and the end of any project, any life.

Yet he is a satiric figure – his vulgar clothes, his rebellious digestive tract, his accent are all mocked in the novel – because he represents the plebian assumption that animal satisfaction and death are all there is. Carlyle called this 'pig morality', and Nabokov finds it equally offensive. In Kinbote's eyes, Gradus kills kings and poets because he is anti-art and does not want specialists of any kind to exist. Reverse the letters of his name and you get 'Sudarg of Bokay', a mirror-maker in Kinbote's Zembla, someone skilled in the art of making the delicate glass objects that Nabokov uses, like Hawthorne in 'The Artist of the Beautiful', as symbols for the fragile but enduring world of art. Gradus tries his hand at the glass business but he, like his grimly realistic, commonsensical cohorts, makes only dark and opaque windows, because he lacks the imagination necessary to see reality in its mirror-shapes or crystalline formations, to see time as reversible, to see identity as infinitely various.

As various critics have pointed out, Shade and Kinbote are in some important senses a study in contrast: the former is a physical misfit, a cheerful agnostic, and a monogamous heterosexual, the latter an accomplished athlete, a Christian apologist, and a promiscuous homosexual, but it is also important to recognize that, 'as befits two aspects of a single creator, Shade and Kinbote have a lot in common'.[7] Their imaginative compact as fellow artists makes them speak with a common voice when they dismiss with helpless laughter vulgar psychologists like Freud, or defend enlightened monarchy against vulgar opportunists like Gradus and his co-conspirators. Nabokov has planted all sorts of clues in the novel to suggest that Shade has created Kinbote, and Gradus, and the whole wild farrago of inspired nonsense his poem occasions. The critical debate about these issues goes on, and will go on, yet there is no particular reason to believe that the novel can be 'figured out' in any definitive way, if only because such metaphors imply that the pleasure of tracing echo and re-echo as one reads and rereads is not the main thing. New crosswords and acrostics are published every day because no one wants to reconsult the solved ones. Presumably John Shade refuses to write the last line of his poem, because like Fyodor in *The Gift*, he has no desire to invoke closure. Charles Kinbote's last entry in the Index is to his own country's 'feigned remoteness', to Zembla, a 'distant northern land', a reference that was to suggest, insisted Nabokov, 'unfinished interrupted life'.[8] *Pale Fire*'s readers are well advised to keep things as open-ended.

There was a great deal of experimental fiction published in the 1960s, particularly in America. John Barth played with various notions of voice in *Lost in the Funhouse: Fiction for Print, Tape, Live Voice*, and in *Giles Goat-Boy* he imagined the whole world as a university in which his eponymous hero must find his way into the belly of the computer controlling the 'West Campus' and grapple there with the mysteries of knowledge and its destructive powers. Joseph Heller's *Catch-22* replayed World War Two in surrealist fantasy terms, as American entrepreneurial capitalism invades the European theatre and reveals the real goals and methods of the war effort. Kurt Vonnegut created his own brand of dystopia in *Cat's Cradle* and *Slaughterhouse Five*. Add to these mainstream novels the drug-induced nightmares of William Burroughs and Charles Bukowski, the stylistic innovations that turn on an idiosyncratic combination of weary laconicism and random violence in fiction by Joan Didion and Susan Sontag, and the now forgotten works of writers like Thomas McGuane (*The Bushwacked Piano*), Richard Brautigan (*Trout Fishing in America*), and other gurus for the young – and the experimental character of the prose written in that ill-mannered, iconoclastic decade becomes clear. Nabokov would have been appalled to hear his name linked with these, but in the 1960s and 1970s he, like these novelists, pushed hard to discover the outer limits of the genre.

Ada provides an interesting example of this testing and experimentation. Nabokov detested science fiction, but situated this novel on a planet called Antiterra, a world with the geography of 'Terra' but its own strange history, and impressed a number of scientifically-oriented critics in the process.[9] His penchant for filtering the world through a single consciousness militated against writing a 'family saga' with a Tolstoyan cast of characters, but he tried his (parodic) hand at it in this novel, and was credited by many with reinventing

the nineteenth-century novel.[10] He generally shunned the novel
of ideas, knowing his gifts lay elsewhere, but in *Ada* his hero
tries to work out a philosophy of time, and argues with Einstein,
Freud, art critics and a host of others who, in Nabokov's view,
should be exposed as frauds. Nabokov may not have succeeded in
surmounting all the obstacles he set himself, but surely no novelist
at his age has ever set out more determinedly to make it new.

The best way to read *Ada*, the first time through anyway, is to skip
the first few pages, a somewhat laboured parody of the opening of
the typical family chronicle, and, beginning with Chapter Four,
read the long and lovingly detailed account of the hero's youth
and young manhood that makes up the first half of the book. Here
is a representative sample of the novel's first section, taken from a
description of one of Van Veen's first encounters with Ada, the girl
who turns out to be his sister and the great love of his life:

> He swore wretchedly in the hopelessness of his bed as he focused
> his swollen senses on the glimpse of her he had engulfed when,
> on their second excursion to the top of the house, she had
> mounted upon a captain's trunk to unhasp a sort of illuminator
> through which one acceded to the roof (even the dog had once
> gone there), and a bracket or something wrenched up her skirt
> and he saw – as one sees some sickening miracle in a Biblical
> fable or a moth's shocking metamorphosis – that the child was
> darkly flossed. He noticed that she seemed to have noticed that
> he had or might have noticed (what he not only noticed but
> retained with tender terror until he freed himself of that vision
> – much later – and in strange ways), and an odd, dull, arrogant
> look passed across her face: her sunken cheeks and fat pale lips
> moved as if she were chewing something, and she emitted a
> yelp of joyless laughter when he, big Van, slipped on a tile
> after wriggling in his turn through the skylight. And in the
> sudden sun, he realized that until then, he, small Van, had
> been a blind virgin, since haste, dust and dusk had obscured
> the mousy charms of his first harlot, so often possessed.
> His sentimental education now went on fast. (65–66)

The passage provides numerous examples of what lies ahead: a
comic account of sexual yearnings and anatomical explorations, a
lexical fussiness ('he noticed that she seemed to have noticed . . . ')
that bestows a mock precision in the context and parodies the

novelist who believes that one more conjunction or clause will enable him to 'capture' reality, a certain looseness in the choice of epithets ('shocking metamorphosis', 'tender terror') that alerts the reader to the fact that in this novel a hyperbolic presentation of both emotion and sensation will systematically flout verisimilitude, and a precision in the delineation of visual detail that shows how it will flaunt it.

The passing allusion to Flaubert's *L'Education sentimentale*, a classic nineteenth-century novel which chronicles the whole complex set of experiences that turn the world of intense adolescent desires into a collection of banal adult regrets, suggests that *Ada* will also be a parody that at the same time pays subtle homage to its forebears. Flaubert's hero, Frédéric Moreau, represents a whole generation of young Frenchmen who participate in the revolutionary hopes of 1848 and their subsequent disappointments; Nabokov's lives on another planet in which the superior individual gets to write his own history. Moreau's great love affair is unrequited, the worship of an ideal that evanesces; Van Veen's is consummated while he is still a young teenager and, having survived a series of comic infidelities and forced separations, endures for decades. Flaubert's novel is a intricate portrayal of the mundane exigencies of everyday life; Nabokov's represents an 'ever-ever land'[11] where there is no obstacle to the fulfilment of any desire and no politics worth bothering about. Since Flaubert, the novel has systematically demystified love and its illusions; in *Ada*, the illusions of love are sustained, magnified, glorified. The series of parallels suggested by a single allusion from a text which features many thousands gives some idea of the density of this extraordinary exercise in erudition.

As scene follows scene, and we learn the details of the relationship of this 'super-imperial couple', a number of things emerge. Most importantly, Nabokov is shown to be one of the century's most acrobatic verbal geniuses, and he has more self-conscious fun in this novel than ever before, playing with words, creating marvellously inventive trilingual puns, exploring a host of rhetorical strategies, and elaborating fantastically complex patterns which reveal themselves to the attentive and the erudite during repeated re-readings. But this approach entails a number of trade-offs. The zany quality of the humour gives the book a lighter quality than some of his earlier work. As importantly, a crucial Nabokov theme, sex is something inexplicably powerful that inevitably gets mere mortals into trouble, has been subjected to the same sort of parodic scrutiny that the classical novel receives. All the hilarious consequences of sexual frustration and satiation are there in *Ada*, but the more ominous effects of the same desires are matters of such oblique allusion, epiphenomena in such a rarefied realm, that they lose some of their power to impress. Jealousy, infidelity, sexual taboo, those crucial players from earlier novels are reduced here to the status of mere counters in the game. There are many references to the pain occasioned by such intense desire, but it too seems, like the grief for Edward King in Milton's 'Lycidas', more a product of the conventions governing the actual writing of the work than something central to the experience of reading it. Readers of American fiction in the 1960s whose taste in fantasy had been schooled by Barth's *Giles Goat-Boy* and Pynchon's *The Crying of Lot 49* found *Ada* curiously weightless because not only did it shun social or political concerns – his fiction had always done that – but because its emotional range had narrowed so drastically as well.

The narrative is so exclusively devoted to Ada and Van, two 'immortals' (they die 'into the finished book'), that the supporting cast acquires a distinctly subordinate status (Lucette, their half-sister, is the only significant exception). Their father is a novelistic caricature, their mother a figure of fun, Van's rivals and Ada's lovers are something out of Boy's Own fiction. Van is as uninterested in the sufferings of others as some of his precursors, but whereas in earlier novels Nabokov uses such incuriosity to ask searching questions about the conflict between aesthetic bliss and imaginative sympathy, in *Ada* he writes a novel in which such an inquiry is itself foregrounded. The novel contains, for example, its own set of literary critical questions about moral significance: 'Was Van's adult incapacity to "shrug" things off only physical or did it "correspond" to some archetypal character of his "undersoul"?' (83).[12] By including such auto-commentary, Nabokov simply took a logical next step, and created a proleptic parody of the ethical high seriousness even the most resolutely comic fiction was to attract in the subject-starved academic criticism of the late twentieth century. Van's cruelty is presented in so many tones and is visited upon such chimerical figures that reading the book as an ethical treatise that earnestly denounces malignity requires one to ignore the extremely various effects of all its felt moments.

Nabokov's approach makes the attempt to posit an authorial

attitude in a book like this extremely arbitrary. Those who are quick to spot the good-natured Henry James parody in the book sometimes seem to assume that a Jamesian novel of subtle hints, ironies that slowly become apparent, complex structures of behaviour that gradually reveal the codes informing them, can be as easily written about a world without a centre of gravity like Antiterra as it can about the social structures James represents in his fiction. But this is not the case, even if Nabokov wanted it to be, and the casual, intermittent parody of such fiction remains just that. Because Nabokov is on record as saying he dislikes Van Veen, some have been tempted to argue that the self-congratulatory snobbery that characterizes many of the conversations between Ada and Van is subtly ironized, as if they were aesthetes *à la* Gilbert Osmond and Madame Merle from *Portrait of a Lady*, but certain kinds of fiction lend themselves better than others to positing the carefully maintained distance necessary for the orchestration of such effects. In *Ada*, the inhuman gamester and the stern moralist are simply two of the many masks Nabokov tries on.

While it seems distinctly odd to praise the novel for its moral recommendations when it is persistently parodies such recommendations and by implication such praise, so too is it difficult to criticize the book for its apparent lapses. The obsession with women as a motley array of fleshy lumps could be a parodic survey of soft porn, the trivializing of most human relations could be a send up of the family chronicle *Ada* pretends to be, the static quality of the characters a joke on the *Bildungsroman*, the wildly overwritten passages could be a compendium of prose styles *à la Ulysses*, and so on. Along with rapturous praise, *Ada* received some very negative reviews when it appeared, and even Nabokov's most faithful supporters have felt obliged to adopt a defensive tone when attempting to justify its excesses. But systematically both those who criticize and those who defend find themselves invoking as criteria novelistic conventions that the novel challenges and undermines.

Rather than praising or condemning *Ada* for what it does not attempt, it might be more fruitful to regard it as one of the decade's most interesting examples of what Northrop Frye defines as Menippean satire, that form in which 'stylized characterization', 'loose-jointed narrative', 'the free play of intellectual fancy', 'the kind of humorous observation that produces caricature', and 'an enormous mass of erudition' figure predominantly.[13] This approach helps explain other feature of the book, something not

seen in Nabokov's work since *The Real Life of Sebastian Knight,* a willingness to forgo his usual strict formal control over his material.
In other works he sometimes made a cameo appearance, as a
figure incomprehensible to the novels' characters, as an anagram
to tease the reader, as a *deus ex machina* content to reveal his own
machinations. He does all this in *Ada,* but in addition for the first
time he brings all his 'strong opinions' to the novel and distributes
them liberally.

The Menippean satirist loves a fight, and Nabokov was particularly fierce in the 1960s with those who have concentrated in their
work on the illnesses of contemporary culture (writers like Thomas
Mann, T. S. Eliot, Sigmund Freud), and in *Ada* both the glancing
and detailed references to these figures make this clear. Yet all the
amusing polemic that results has tended to obscure the important
similarities between him and his modernist forebears. Take Mann,
for example, who is mocked in *Ada* and elsewhere in Nabokov's
work. Just as in *Lolita* Nabokov gives a new twist to the theme
of 'Death in Venice', a fascination with sensual beauty that plays
havoc with the aesthetic and the moral sense, so too in *Ada* does
he write a comic version of *The Magic Mountain,* by making Van
Veen a mocking philosophical quester as cut off from the world
of contemporary concerns and world history as Hans Castorp in
the quasi-timelessness of his sanatorium. Mann uses his novel to
work out a subjective theory of time that turns on the difference
between our normal sense of clock time and a sense of individual
moments, with a view to propounding a new view of history,
both personal and political. Nabokov does something remarkably
similar in Part Four of his novel. The charming, Bergson-inspired
meander called 'The Texture of Time' is less thought-provoking
than Mann's meditation, but it is also a lot more fun. One might
even argue that Nabokov's insistence that he discovered nothing
but clichés in Mann's work is a self-defensive, Bloomian swerve
away from confronting modernism's most original treatment of
Ada's subject: the 'awareness of living on a duality or plurality of
levels'.[14] Pound's and Eliot's quests for a unity that exists beyond
the mere succession of moments are also germane here, but again
Nabokov's anti-modernist polemics – he routinely insisted that
Pound and Eliot were fakes, and pronounced himself mystified
by their general appeal – has discouraged any investigation of the
links.

The quarrel with Freud is an old one (Nabokov made fun of his doctrines in a Russian *émigré* newspaper in the 1930s) but *Ada* is his most detailed account of his revulsion for Freudian psychiatry. In addition to the obvious reasons for Nabokov's attitude towards psychoanalysis – Freud's insistence that even the most fiercely independent creative genius is as subservient as the humble ignoramus to the workings of his unconscious, the crude symbolism of dream interpretation, the idea that a positivist science of the mind can teach us anything useful about something that is quintessentially mysterious – Nabokov's deep antipathy also stems from Freud's claim that 'man at his best and man at his worst is subject to a common set of explanations: that good and evil grow from a common process', his refusal to consider humanity's moral qualities in isolation. Freud's deprecation of romantic love ('Even to-day [in 1912], love, too, is in essence as animal as it ever was') [15] cannot have endeared him to Nabokov either. And all the continuities 'between man and the animal kingdom, between dreams and unreason on one side and waking rationality on the other, between madness and sanity . . . between primitive and civilized man' [16] that are essential to Freudian thought strike Nabokov as glib or misleading or simply preposterous.

In *Ada* Nabokov concentrates on Freudian dream interpretation, and his hero insists that 'the mental and moral faculties of the dreamer', those features of the unconscious that manifest themselves in everyday life, are certain indications of the primitive, retarded level of this absurd, amusing, but ultimately negligible aspect of human existence. Van Veen gives some hilarious lectures on the subject, and readers can judge for themselves whether he succeeds in making his case as well as Swift, Voltaire and Sterne do in their attacks on philosophers and pedants. Here is a typical passage:

> when a teashop humorist says that a little conical titbit with a comical cherry on top resembles this or that (titters in the audience) he is turning a pink cake into a pink breast (tempestuous laughter) in a fraise-like frill or frilled phrase (silence). Both objects are real, they are not interchangeable, not tokens of something else, say, of Walter Raleigh's decapitated trunk still topped by the image of his wetnurse (one lone chuckle). (386)

My own sense is that his method of arguing from vividly imagined examples gains Nabokov a number of dazzling minor victories,

but leaves some of the main questions untouched. Crudely symbolic interpretations deserve to be caricatured, but there is nothing crude about Freud's view of the unconsious. For Freud, the
unconscious is:

> one or more well-articulated systems of beliefs and desires,
> systems that are just as complex, sophisticated, and inter-
> nally consistent as the normal adult's conscious beliefs and
> desires . . . What is novel in Freud's view of the unconscious
> is his claim that our unconscious selves are not dumb, sullen,
> lurching brutes, but rather the intellectual peers of our conscious
> selves, possible conversational partners for those selves. As Rieff
> puts it, 'Freud democratized genius by giving everyone a creative
> unconscious'.[17]

It is this aspect of Freud's thought that goes unchallenged in
Nabokov, but for those predisposed to sympathize with his view
of Freud's theories, no discussion of what Freud actually meant
by the unconscious will matter much, and *Ada*'s portrayal of the
'Viennese quack' will constitute a 'final pronouncement' in this
area as well. If, on Antiterra, Bergson's metaphoric musings can
be used to 'disprove' Einstein's concept of time, and Nabokov can
be characterized as a writer who made a seminal contribution to
philosophic thought on this question,[18] then he can certainly be
cited as a psychologist whose insights have superseded Freud's as
well. To say, as the American pragmatist Richard Rorty has recently
done,[19] that Nabokov had no interest in propounding or skill in
constructing philosophical arguments will seem unexceptionable
to most. Why on earth should he have had? We don't criticize
Joyce for not writing fiery prophetic novels about a new kind
of human relationship, Lawrence for refusing to try his hand at
polyglot puns, Proust for ignoring the rise of labour unions in
nineteenth-century France, or Zola for not penning subtle analyses
of beauty and nostalgia. Anyone who can force readers to revise
their ideas about the relationship between literature and reality,
create sentences like the ones in *The Gift* or *Lolita*, and delight as
consummately as he does in *Pale Fire* or his published interviews,
has done all that can reasonably be asked of one writer.

Look at the Harlequins!, Nabokov's last published novel (he was
working something called 'The Original of Laura' when he died),
represents an appropriate conclusion for the final, self-regarding

phase of his fiction. In *Ada* Nabokov anticipated the critics' response by including his own review as a blurb (as Barth had done in his *Giles Goat-Boy* published in 1962). In his final novel he challenges critics to call him narcissistic, introverted, and obsessed with the theme of writing, by creating a book in which he is self-consciously all of these things. Nabokov gives his narrator the name of his creator – Vadim Vadimovich is the normal way of pronouncing Vladimir Vladimirovich in Russian – and a bibliography that reads like Nabokov's own works scrambled by a drunken librarian.

In some ways it is very much a novel appropriate to its decade: in an influential summary of America in the 1970s, *The Culture of Narcissism*, Christopher Lasch notes how popular the confessional mode was at that time for well-known writers who were keen to parade a self before the public. He differentiates between two sorts of confession: 'the objectification of one's own experience, as psychiatric studies of narcissism have shown, makes it possible for "the deep sources of grandiosity and exhibitionism – after being appropriately aim-inhibited, tamed and neutralized – [to] find access" to reality'; and the mere catalogue of undigested experience, often salacious details to satisfy a public hungry for scandal, that represents a less fruitful (and more cynical) sort of self-disclosure'.[20] The writer whose autobiography, *Speak, Memory*, tells us almost nothing about his personal life was not likely to write either type of confession at an age when he guarded his privacy even more fiercely now that he was famous, but a parody of such a book gave him a vehicle in which he could make fun of both kinds of confession, *and* explore other possibilities in the self-reflexive mode of which he was the master. Thus *Look at the Harlequins!* turns on the narcissist's nightmare occasioned when the act of writing allows no detachment, and features a beleaguered narrator with a shadow self that gives him no peace, that makes him act out his life as if it belongs to someone else.

The result is a Nabokovian text that repeatedly presents laboriously contrived 'distress' in a jocular tone that distances and diminishes the events narrated, all the while ingeniously incorporating them in a hectic version of Nabokov's anti-life, a grotesquely distorted version of the one he actually lived. Much is made, for example, of Vadim's problem with imagining space swivel as he turns at the half way point of an imaginary walk. This inability causes him extraordinary anxiety, but the mock serious tone militates against the reader's taking it as anything but a joke. The lives of many Russian (and American) writers have been as wracked by jealousy as Nabokov's was free of it; therefore he makes poor Vadim the victim of such pangs, but the object of his envy is his own creator, to whose work his is constantly being compared. The result is an extraordinarily dense book, filled with an array of allusions to Nabokov's life and art, twisted out of true by his strange mirror, but a book that is at the same time remarkably thin. It is as if Joyce had chosen to make his last novel a parody called *Stephen Underachiever,* or Dostoevsky had concluded his career with the pseudo-biography (*Memoirs from a Mousehole?*) of one of his epigones. But for those who have made a life work of Nabokovian arcana, here presumably is God's plenty.[21]

Some critics have suggested that *Look at the Harlequins!* dramatizes Nabokov's alienation from an entire *oeuvre,* and his own isolation, but his serenely self-confident pronouncements in interviews when such subjects came up suggest that this cannot be the whole answer. Is *Look at the Harlequins!* Nabokov's attempt to question common assumptions about an autonomous thing called a self that can comment authoritatively on its origins, continuity, unity, and uniqueness? As we saw in our discussion of *Pale Fire,* the subject of a range of postmodernist novels is the decentering of the very notion of 'subject', the systematic interrogation of concepts like autonomous, authority, origin, continuity, unity, and uniqueness.[22] The pastiche of titles, the coming to life of clichéic responses to his work (for those who thought that anyone who could write a book like *Lolita* must be a paedophile, Nabokov has his stand-in tempted by nymphets), the removal of the boundaries between fiction and autobiography, the confusion about identities and the nature of the past that results, these would seem to make *Look at the Harlequins!* the ideal Nabokov novel for the postmodernist critic. (Even the repetition, the flatness, the tediousness of great chunks of the novel should not bother such critics; studies of literary postmodernism usually quote liberally from texts and include detailed summaries of them but eschew evaluation.) Yet surely such critics are going to have problems with the self-satisfied quality of the interrogation, the fact that the whole book turns on the assumption that there is such a thing as an author who effortlessly soars above the mundane concerns with self-definition that afflict lesser mortals.

Take the ending, for example, in which closure is invoked, the interrogation concluded, the questions answered. A figure identified only as 'You' enters Vadim's hospital room, and promptly alleviates his 'metaphysical' concerns, sorts out his identity, and promises to nurse him back to health. Vadim is reluctant to tell his readers too much about her – 'Reality would be only adulterated if I now started to narrate what shall never, never be ferreted out by a matter-of-fact, father-of-muck, mucking biograffitist' (179) – we are told, but he is clearly on the way to being cured, and to being conflated with the 'incomparably greater, healthier, and crueler' (89) writer who has been haunting his life. When Nabokov wrote the novel, he was greatly distressed by what he had seen of Andrew Field's biography, *Nabokov: His Life in Part*, in proof, because of the many errors it contained, because Field had insisted on using sources whom Nabokov regarded as unreliable or irrelevant, and because Field refused to give his subject the editorial 'last word' he had been promised. 'You' turns out to be a stand-in for the dedicatee of Nabokov's novels, the person addressed in his autobiography, the author's muse, secretary, and chief admirer, his wife Véra. But we are told nothing about her: Vadim's disclosures have been a nightmare born of a confusion between life and art, the story and the confession. The master of Montreux would never stoop to making himself or his loved ones so public, so vulnerable. The self-examination the modernists took seriously, the breakdown of autonomous notions of that self the postmodernists celebrated in their angular meditations – these are finally as distinct from Nabokov's concerns here as the moralizing tract or the naturalistic study of the effects of the environment upon the individual. In the end he was still intent on making it new, still eager to go his own way.

If one examines the careers of many great novelists, one often detects a certain willed, self-conscious quality in the productions of their mature years. Henry James famously criticized Dickens for digging out his late novels 'with a spade and a pick-ax', and critics of James have identified a laboured quality in his work by dividing it up into eras called James I, James II, and James the Great Pretender. If one considers Richardson's *Sir Charles Grandison*, Conrad's *The Rover*, Woolf's *The Years*, Lawrence's *The Plumed Serpent*, Goncharov's *The Precipice*, Tolstoy's *Resurrection*, Turgenev's *Virgin Soil*, Fitzgerald's *The Last Tycoon*, Hemingway's *Across the River and Into the Trees*, Bellow's *A Theft*, and Norman Mailer's *Egyptian Evenings*, one gets a sense of how variously this phenomenon manifests itself. (The novels produced by Trollope, H. G. Wells and Sherwood Anderson after their best work had been done suggest that the phase can be indefinitely extended.) These novels are all characterized by a self-consciousness that obtrudes itself, by unconscious lapses into self-parody, and by a sense of having been produced by someone who was thinking of him- or herself as an important writer, or as a writer with a daily word limit to reach, while the text was being transcribed. For the novelists in the list cited above the resulting problems can create the impression of a work written against the grain, but for writers like Nabokov the effect is simply to add one more level of complexity. After all, has he not made a whole career by deliberately challenging the limits of the genre he helped redefine?

Seen from this perspective, *Look at the Harlequins!* can, of course, be recuperated as the parody of a self-parody, the flattened characters, manneristic style, all redeemed as an alert exercise in mock self-mockery, but such an argument is not likely to convince a posterity with a limited amount of reading time on its hands. And why should an author's intentionally imposed limitations matter when decisions about how to read a given work are being taken? Once give the self-parody argument its head and all the works listed above, not to mention most of late Wordsworth and Tennyson, Hugo and Longfellow, Nekrasov and Nadson should be read, not as curiosities of failed imagination and advancing age, studied only as a form of penal servitude by graduate students desperate for a topic, but as energetic exercises in self-imitation, zestful celebrations of the emptiness that accompanies any overly ingenious attempt to find a new voice. The problem is that no one besides the jaded academician, hungry for new texts and approaches, will credit such arguments. A man who has performed philanthropic deeds all his life while harbouring a secret hatred for humanity can be deemed a 'good' person in most ways that matter. In the same way, a novel that does such a convincing job of seeming preeningly narcissistic and self-indulgently hermetic that it puts off everyone, even if it is revealed later to be, when held up to the light a certain way, a parody of a parody or a tribute to married love as a force that transcends time, or some combination of the two,[23] such a novel will remain for most what they first took it to be. And this is emphatically not a question of the general reader's lack of imaginative energy or erudition, of not reading carefully or well enough: even if all the allusions in the novel were painstakingly decoded, no one but the Nabokovians, and not all of them at that, would care.

7

Conclusion

So where to put the final accent? The *topos* of modesty about reductive commentary whose only purpose is to send the reader back to the texts, often invoked at this point in critical studies, is particularly appropriate in the case of Nabokov. Any emphasis on the complex quality of his art, because it tends to make him sound excessively cerebral, offers a poor substitute for the actual experience of reading him. Nabokov will be remembered, not because he supplied critics with a lot to write about, but because he wrote extraordinary sentences and used them to say perceptive and amusing things about our world. The pleasures of the texture will continue to be savoured by lovers of sensuous linguistic patterns, those of the text by readers who want fiction to interrogate and modify their understanding of reality. Readers who believe that literature is produced by people whose brains are in some special way different from their own will always find in his work a very distinctive kind of intelligent pleasure. And not only in the novels. He once described in an interview his American students taking an exam as 'the great fraternity of C—, backbone of the nation, steadily scribbling on'. He concluded a hilarious (and rather cruel) denunciation of one of his critics: 'And he will be read, he will be quoted, he will be filed in great libraries, next to my arbors and mists!'[1] The polemics with Maurice Girodias, *Lolita*'s publisher, or Edmund Wilson, in a famous dispute about Nabokov's translation of *Eugene Onegin*, are small masterpieces of wit and invective. In short, Nabokov's handiwork often reads like others' masterwork.

Any commentary on the meaning and value of his novels, even while it advances certain arguments and offers various criteria by which the novels might be judged, must cheerfully admit to their ability to sustain a range of readings and to encourage different responses over time, and such multiplicity should augur well for Nabokov's future in academia. Recent developments in literary criticism have tended to downplay the importance of the author and literary genius, to depreciate notions of the creative imagination or inspiration as dead metaphors, and to dispute the subservience to authority implicit in the hierarchical notion of a 'great writer' who has important things to tell attentive readers. If this trend continues, those whose novels seem inextricably bound up with such notions may well, like so many old circus performers, be rudely expelled from the new canon. No matter. When Nabokov says, at the end of one of his lectures, 'The work with this group has been a particularly pleasant association between the fountain of my voice and a garden of ears – some open, others closed, many very receptive, a few merely ornamental, but all of them human and divine',[2] he tells us everything we need to know about himself as a teacher: the hierarchical relationship is there because order is essential for communication; the students have their rôle to play, yet his respect for their human otherness does not depend on their willingness to play it. So too with the novelist: he enjoys his mastery of a sympathetic readership but he knows that not everyone will want to belong to it. Those who do should guarantee Nabokov a richly deserved posterity.

Notes

1 Introduction

1. See *Strong Opinions* (New York: McGraw Hill, 1974) pp. 51–52, 302 (hereafter *SO*).
2. See John Bayley, *Selected Essays* (Cambridge: Cambridge University Press, 1984), p. 175.
3. *SO*, p. 98.
4. *SO*, p. 184 (see also *SO*, p. 155). Malcolm Bradbury's lucid distinctions between two views of postmodernism have helped organize the argument in this paragraph. See his *Saul Bellow* (London: Methuen, 1982), pp. 16–18.
5. *Contingency, Irony, and Solidarity* (Cambridge: Cambridge University Press, 1989), p. 161, n. 26.
6. *SO*, p. 114.

2 Lives of a Young *Émigré*: *Mary, Glory,* and *The Gift*

1. All page references are to the American hardback editions, except where indicated: the page reference of the Russian original precedes the one to the translation.
2. See Arthur C. Danto, *Nietzsche as Philosopher* (New York: Macmillan, 1965), pp. 209–13.
3. *Speak, Memory: An Autobiography Revisited* (New York: Putnam, 1966), p. 219.
4. For a useful summary of the distinguishing features of the Romantic movement, see Cedric Watts, *A Preface to Keats* (London: Longman, 1985), pp. 74–75.
5. Brian Boyd, *Vladimir Nabokov: The Russian Years* (Princeton, N.J.: Princeton University Press, 1990), p. 361. The theme of the transcendent realm is explored in Boyd's two-volume biography and in Vladimir Alexandrov's *Nabokov's Otherworld* (Princeton, N.J.: Princeton University Press, 1991), two recent publications that should prove indispensable for readers of Nabokov's work.
6. Those interested in Nabokov's life at Cambridge should consult *Speak, Memory*, Chapter 13, and *Nabokov: The Russian Years*, pp. 166–95, but there is also the delightful 'Universitetskaya poema [University

Poem]', *Sovremennye Zapiski*, 33 (1927), pp. 223–54, which tells in sixty-three neo-Pushkinian stanzas the story of an affair between a young Russian student and a local girl. Social teas, cramming for exams, talking politics with the locals – these events are all rendered with a mastery that suggests how skilled a narrative poet Nabokov was, a suggestion that was confirmed in 'Pale Fire'.

7. *The Nabokov–Wilson Letters: Correspondence Between Vladimir Nabokov and Edmund Wilson 1940–1977*, ed. Simon Karlinsky (New York: Harper and Row, 1979), p. 96.

8. See John Bayley, *Selected Essays*, p. 156.

9. *Nabokov–Wilson Letters*, p. 240.

10. *Journey to Arzrum* (*Sochineniya v trex tomax*) (Moscow: Khudozhestvennaya literatura, 1986), III, p. 409.

11. *SO*, p. 103.

12. 'The Dénouement of *The Government Inspector*', *Sobranie Sochineniy v semi tomakh*, ed. S. I. Mashinskoy *et al.* (Moscow: Khudozhestvennaya Literatura, 1967), IV, p. 410.

13. *SO*, p. 95.

14. *Lectures on Literature* (New York: Harcourt Brace Jovanovich/Bruccoli Clark, 1980), p. 64. See *Contingency, Irony, and Solidarity*, pp. 147–48: 'The pursuit of private perfection is a perfectly reasonable aim for some writers – writers like Plato, Heidegger, Proust, and Nabokov, who share certain talents. Serving human liberty is a perfectly reasonable aim for other writers – people like Dickens, Mill, Dewey, Orwell, Habermas, and Rawls, who share others. There is no point in trying to grade these different pursuits on a single scale by setting up factitious kinds called "literature" or "art" or "writing"; nor is there any point in trying to synthesize them'.

15. Many Nabokov critics see the treatment of Chernyshevsky in *The Gift* rather differently. Brian Boyd argues that 'Because [Fyodor] considers his subject afresh, as a unique person and not the saintly icon of the progressives, he can detect the fatal flaw everywhere in Chernyshevsky's destiny that reduces all his hopes to nothing. . . . What at first seems a mocking hostility on fate's part and Fyodor's proves to be an unrelenting focus on what is unique in the man, and therefore irreplaceable, vulnerable, frail'. He adds that Alexander Dolinin (*Vladimir Nabokov: Izbrannoe* [Moscow: Raduga, 1990]) 'demonstrates conclusively V.N.'s fidelity to the documentary evidence' (*Nabokov: The Russian Years*, pp. 458, 578, n. 4. But the fact that Nabokov has an actual source for all the things he says about Chernyshevsky does not make Chapter Four an authentic portrait of Chernyshevsky's 'uniqueness'. Professor Dolinin himself admits that Nabokov's character 'of course treats his material freely enough', and that his account includes 'both inaccuracies and deliberate changes' (*Izbrannoe*, p. 622). And one can be faithful to the documentary evidence and still misrepresent one's subject, for example, by omitting references to material that does not support one's particular view. Dolinin's extremely detailed and helpful annotations to this extraordinarily allusive chapter establish only

the first kind of fidelity. See my *Vladimir Nabokov: A Critical Study of the Novels* (Cambridge: Cambridge University Press, 1984), pp. 64–92, for a more detailed account of these issues.

It is interesting that the Chernyshevsky biography has mostly been ignored by those who have written about him since *The Gift* was published. These are people who are not in the least blinkered by a revolutionary religiosity in their view of him, and who manage to present a balanced account of his character and achievements without resorting to Nabokov's inspired caricature. See, for example, Isaiah Berlin, *Russian Thinkers*, ed. Henry Hardy and Aileen Kelly (London: The Hogarth Press, 1978); William F. Woehrlin, *Chernyshevskii: The Man and the Journalist* (Cambridge, Mass.: Harvard University Press, 1971); and Irina Paperno, *Chernyshevsky and the Age of Realism: A Study in the Semiotics of Behavior* (Plao Alto, Calif.: Stanford University Press, 1988). Even Vasiliy Rozanov, whom one cannot imagine to be a writer more different from Chernyshevsky, conveys in a couple of pages in *Solitaria* more intuitive understanding of the Russian radical than Nabokov does in his long chapter (see *Solitaria*, trans. S. S. Koteliansky (Westport, Conn.: Greenwood Press, 1979), pp. 62–65.

16.   *The Wit and Humor of Oscar Wilde*, ed. Alvin Redman (New York: Dover Publications, 1959), p. 229.
17.   Quoted in Boyd, *Nabokov: The Russian Years*, p. 54.
18.   *The Bodley Head G.K. Chesterton* (London: The Bodley Head, 1985), p. 262.
19.   In the original these last sentences are also rhymed, but the second line reads 'For visions there are also no mortal postponements', and *Dar* concludes: 'the extended phantom of existence shows blue beyond the bounds of the page, like tomorrow's clouds, – and the line is not finished'.
20.   See *SO*, p. 153.
21.   *Eugene Onegin*, revn. edn, trans. with a commentary by Vladimir Nabokov (Princeton, N.J.: Princeton University Press, 1975), III, p. 241.

3   Studies in Obsession: *The Defense, The Eye, Laughter in the Dark, and Despair*

1.   *The Complete Psychological Works*, ed. and trans. James Strachey (London: Hogarth, 1953), XX, p. 139, IV, pp. 212–13, X, p. 241.
2.   *Speak, Memory*, p. 38.
3.   'Review of *The Defence*', *The New Statesman*, 6 November 1964, p. 703.
4.   *Worlds in Regression: Some Novels of Vladimir Nabokov* (Ann Arbor, Mich.: Ardis, 1985), pp. 83–92.
5.   Brian Boyd, 'The Problem of Pattern: Nabokov's *Defense*', *Modern Fiction Studies*, 33 (1987), pp. 575–604. The article is summarized in Boyd, *Nabokov: The Russian Years*, pp. 333–39.
6.   *Nabokov: The Russian Years*, p. 339.

7. The fifth sentence in *Soglyadatay* concludes: '[t]o come to no conclusions, simply to stare'; Nabokov cut this and added epithets like 'vitreous' and 'bloodshot' in the English translation. All the details about the underwear on the clothesline are also additions; the original refers only to 'heartrending meetings at night'.

8. See, for example, Alfred Appel's comments in his delightful study of Nabokov and the movies, *Nabokov's Dark Cinema* (New York: Oxford University Press, 1974), p. 262.

9. This passage does not exist in *Kamera Obskura*, which was substantially reworked by Nabokov when he translated it.

10. Sigmund Freud, *Civilization and Its Discontents* (London: Hogarth Press, 1963), p. 50.

11. Quoted in Boyd, *Nabokov: The Russian Years*, p. 438.

12. I have drawn here on John Kucich's discussion of villainy in Dickens; see *Excess and Restraint in the Novels of Charles Dickens* (Athens, Ga.: University of Georgia Press, 1981), pp. 59–104.

13. *Contingency, Irony, and Solidarity*, pp. 176–77. For a detailed discussion of this question, see Elaine Scarry, *The Body in Pain: The Making and Unmaking of the World* (New York: Oxford University Press, 1985).

14. A. D. Nuttall, *'Crime and Punishment': Murder as Philosophic Experiment* (Edinburgh: Scottish Academic Press for Sussex University Press, 1978), p. 101.

15. *A Treatise of Human Nature*, ed. T. H. Green and T. H. Grose (London: n.p., 1886), II, p. 195.

16. Nuttall, *'Crime and Punishment'*, p. 101.

17. Nabokov's Russian publisher, Petropolis, refused to print the account of Hermann's sexual fantasies.

18. In *Otchayanie* the last words of this line are repeated: 'Zamyslil. Ya. Pobeg.' ('Contemplated. I. Flight.') The inversion of the subject and the verb is perfectly normal in Russian, and the repetition nicely recreates Hermann's solemn, deliberate intonations, as he tries to plant hints in the head of his empty-headed wife.

19. In *Otchayanie*, Nabokov calls Dostoevsky 'the Russian Pinkerton', an allusion to Allan Pinkerton (1819–1884), the founder of a famous US private detective agency.

20. *After Bakhtin: Essays on Fiction and Criticism* (London and New York: Routledge & Kegan Paul, 1990), pp. 59–60.

21. *Problems of Dostoevsky's Poetics* ed. and trans. Caryl Emerson (Minn.: University of Minnesota Press, 1984), p. 104.

22. *Problems of Dostoevsky's Poetics*, p. 166.

4 Experiments in Mid-Career: *Invitation to a Beheading, The Real Life of Sebastian Knight,* and *Bend Sinister*

1. Entry for 21 November 1911, *Diaries: 1910–1913*, ed. Max Brod, trans. Joseph Kresh (New York: Schocken, 1948).

2. See Johnson, *Worlds in Regression*, pp. 31–46, for a outstanding analysis of Nabokov's linguistic brilliance.

3. *SO*, p. 45.
4. *Biography: Fiction, Fact and Form* (London: Macmillan, 1984), p. 104.
5. Malcolm Bradbury, 'The Telling Life: Some Thoughts on Literary Biography', in *The Troubled Face of Biography*, ed. Eric Homberger and John Charmley (London: Macmillan, 1988), p. 133.
6. *Drugie berega* [*Other Shores*] (New York: Chekhov, 1954), p. 8.
7. The argument in this paragraph is indebted to the discussion of learned wit in D. W. Jefferson, '*Tristram Shandy* and the Tradition of Learned Wit', *Essays in Criticism*, 1 (1951), pp. 225–48. A. D. Nuttall pointed out in private correspondence the link between Nabokov and the tradition of learned wit.
8. Jefferson, '*Tristram Shandy*', pp. 238, 239.
9. See *Criticism and Ideology: A Study in Marxist Literary Theory* (London: Verso, 1976), p. 137.

5 The Morality of the Aesthete: *Lolita*

1. *The Confessions of Jean-Jacques Rousseau* (New York: Random House, 1945), p. 88.
2. Quoted in Bertrand Russell, *History of Western Philosophy* (London: George Allen & Unwin, 1946), p. 665.
3. This sort of extravagant conceit has suggested for some readers a Poe-like 'touch of necrophilia' and the 'possibility of violence' (Leona Toker, *Nabokov: The Mystery of Literary Structures* (Ithaca: Cornell University Press), p. 213. The reference to Poe is apt, given his omnipresence in *Lolita*, but his lugubrious brand of hysterical passion seems different in kind from Humbert's humorous yet poignant hyperbole.
4. *Literature Against Itself: Literary Ideas in Modern Society* (Chicago: University of Chicago Press, 1979), p. 8.
5. *Vladimir Nabokov: Selected Letters 1940–1977*, ed. Dimitri Nabokov and Matthew J. Bruccoli (New York: Harcourt Brace Jovanovich/Bruccoli Clark Layman, 1989), p. 399.
6. Quoted in Stephen Jay Gould, *The Flamingo's Smile: Reflections in Natural History* (New York: W. W. Norton, 1985), p. 155.
7. See A. D. Nuttall's fascinating account of the significance of this sort of hesitation in writers as diverse as Euripides, Shakespeare, and Dostoevsky, in '*Crime and Punishment*', pp. 120–22. Other links between Nabokov and Dostoevsky are suggested in Melvin Seidel, 'Nabokov and Dostoevsky', *Contemporary Literature*, 13 (1972), pp. 423–44.
8. See Nuttall, '*Crime and Punishment*', p. 55.
9. *The Enchanter*, trans Dimitri Nabokov (New York: Putnam, 1986), p. 92.
10. Presumably Nabokov left the story unpublished because he found it crude in similar ways. Yet practically every sentence in it, as Gennady Barabtarlo has recently shown ('Those Who Favor Fire',

Russian Literature Triquarterly, 24 (1991), pp. 89–112), is packed full of linguistic ingenuity, the 'wayside murmur' of hidden themes, and the whole elaborate Nabokovian paraphernalia that came as readily to him as stylistic austerity did to Chekhov or Hemingway. By itself though, this ingenuity is far more compelling when Nabokov uses it to create complex characters and situations.

11. *SO*, p. 75.

12. *The Dialogic Imagination: Four Essays*, ed. Michael Holquist, trans. Caryl Emerson and Michael Holquist (Austin, Texas and London: University of Texas Press, 1981), p. 403.

13. Humbert's theory of narrative, such as it is, anticipates the efforts of recent theorists to identify plot development with male arousal and orgasm. For him and for them, female sexual pleasure does not come into it. Susan Winnett protests against 'the gender bias of contemporary narratology' in 'Coming Unstrung: Women, Men, Narrative, and Principles of Pleasure', *PMLA*, 105, 3 (May 1990), pp. 505–18.

14. See Christina Tekiner, 'Time in *Lolita*', *Modern Fiction Studies*, 25 (1979), pp. 463–69, and Nabokov's comments in the interview with Douglas M. Davis, *National Observer*, 29 June 1964, p. 17.

15. 'We Need One Another', in *Phoenix*, ed. Edward McDonald (London: Heinemann, 1936), p. 193.

16. In effect, such conclusions show that moral relativism can coexist with a very conservative set of ethical principles. Just how conservative Nabokov is on such questions becomes clear if we compare Humbert on morality and aesthetics to someone like Chesterton. In 'The Ethics of Elfland' he criticizes the aesthetes for being unwilling 'to pay for their pleasure in any sort of symbolic sacrifice', and goes on: 'Surely one might pay for extraordinary joy in ordinary morals. Oscar Wilde said that sunsets were not valued because we could not pay for sunsets. But Oscar Wilde was wrong; we can pay for sunsets. We can pay for them by not being Oscar Wilde' (*G. K. Chesterton*, p. 263).

17. J. Hillis Miller, Vincent B. Leitch, Barbara Johnson, Christopher Norris, and Jonathan Culler, quoted in John M. Ellis, *Against Deconstruction* (Princeton, N.J.: Princeton University Press, 1989), pp. 68–69, 124.

6 Metafictions: *Pale Fire, Ada,* and *Look at the Harlequins!*

1. See Linda Hutcheon, *The Politics of Postmodernism*, pp. 10–11, 43, for a helpful list of such definitions, as well as the definitions of Michael Bell, *The Sentiment of Reality: Truth of Feeling in the European Novel* (London: George Allen & Unwin, 1983), p. 176, and John McGowan, *Postmodernism and its Critics* (Ithaca, N.Y.: Cornell University Press, 1991), p. 12.

2. Terry Eagleton, *Literary Theory* (Oxford: Basil Blackwell, 1983), p. 133.

3. This should presumably be 'on flagstones', but in a poem where 'life everlasting' can be 'based on a misprint', one is wary of emending Nabokov's text.

4. *Lectures on Literature*, p. 374.

5. See Eagleton, *Literary Theory*, p. 131.

6. See the splendidly detailed study by Priscilla Meyer, *Find What the Sailor has Hidden: Vladimir Nabokov's 'Pale Fire'* (Middletown, Conn.: Wesleyan University Press, 1988).

7. Rorty, *Contingency, Irony, Solidarity*, p. 165. Boyd usefully catalogues the differences in *Vladmir Nabokov: The American Years* (Princeton, N.J.: Princeton University Press), p. 446; Alexandrov discusses in detail the resemblances between Shade and Nabokov, *Nabokov's Otherworld*, pp. 192–202.

8. *Nabokov: The American Years*, p. 464.

9. See, for example, N. Katherine Hayles, *The Cosmic Web: Scientific Field Models and Literary Strategies in the Twentieth Century* (Ithaca, N.Y.: Cornell University Press), pp. 111–37.

10. See Fred Kaplan, 'Victorian Modernist: Fowles and Nabokov', *Journal of Narrative Technique*, 3 (1973), pp. 108–20.

11. 'Nabokov in Embryo', *Time*, 24 January 1969, p. 59.

12. In *Snow White*, which appeared two years before *Ada*, Donald Barthelme has fun with a similar device, a questionnaire that asks readers half way through his novel about themes, how they like the book so far, and whether it has a metaphysical dimension for them.

13. *Anatomy of Criticism: Four Essays* (Princeton, N.J.: Princeton University Press, 1957), pp. 309–12.

14. Charles Taylor, *Sources of the Self: The Making of the Modern Identity* (Cambridge, Mass.: Harvard University Press, 1989), p. 480.

15. Sigmund Freud, *Collected Papers*, ed. and trans. James Strachey, vol. IV (London: Hogarth Press, 1925), p. 215.

16. Jerome Bruner, 'Freud and the Image of Man', *Partisan Review*, 23, 3 (1956), pp. 344–46.

17. Richard Rorty, *Essays on Heidegger and Others: Philosophical Papers* (Cambridge: Cambridge University Press, 1991), p. 149.

18. See Boyd, *Nabokov's 'Ada': The Place of Consciousness*, p. 243, n. 2. Actually, far from imagining that he was refuting Einstein, Bergson thought the new physics complemented and supported his own work. See A. R. Lacey, *Bergson* (London and New York: Routledge & Kegan Paul, 1989), pp. 59–66. Boyd also suggests that 'Nabokov's analysis of the concept of the future [in *Ada*] seems sounder than the work of most philosophers' (p. 237, n. 11).

19. *Contingency, Irony, and Solidarity*, p. 173.

20. *The Culture of Narcissism: American Life in an Age of Diminishing Expectations* (New York: Norton, 1979), pp. 48–49.

21. Alexandrov admits that 'Auto-allusions grow in frequency through time in Nabokov's *oeuvre* and become the dominant feature of *Look at the Harlequins!*', but argues: 'Because such textual echoes have obvious thematic functions and are not merely the author's private winks to himself, it follows that the works in which they appear have to be

read in terms of each other' (*Nabokov's Otherworld*, p. 234). My point is that the themes themselves have become the 'author's private winks to himself'.

22. See, for example, Linda Hutcheon, *A Poetics of Postmodernism: History, Theory, Fiction* (New York and London: Routledge & Kegan Paul, 1988), p. 57.
23. Brian Boyd makes an ingenious case for such a reading; see *Nabokov: The American Years*, pp. 623–42.

7 Conclusion

1. *SO*, pp. 22, 307.
2. *Lectures on Literature*, p. 382.

Select Bibliography

MAJOR WORKS BY VLADIMIR NABOKOV

Novels

Mashen'ka [*Mary*] (Berlin: Slovo, 1926, New York: McGraw-Hill, 1970, and London: Weidenfeld and Nicolson, 1971).

Korol', Dama, Valet [*King, Queen, Knave*] (Berlin: Slovo, 1928, New York: McGraw-Hill, and London: Weidenfeld and Nicolson, 1968).

Zashchita Luzhina [*The Defense*] (Berlin: Slovo, 1930, New York: Putnam, and London: Weidenfeld and Nicolson, 1964).

Podvig [*Glory*] (Paris: Sovremennye Zapiski, 1932, New York: McGraw-Hill, 1971, London: Weidenfeld and Nicolson, 1972).

Kamera Obskura [*Camera Obscura*] (Berlin: Sovremennye Zapiski, 1932, London: John Long, 1936) and *Laughter in the Dark* (Indianopolis and New York: Bobbs-Merrill, 1938).

Otchyanie [*Despair*] (Berlin: Petropolis, 1936, New York: Putnam, 1966, and London: John Long, 1937).

Soglyadatay [*The Eye*] (Berlin: Russkie Zapiski, 1938, New York: Phaedra, 1965, and London: Weidenfeld and Nicolson, 1966).

Priglashenie na kazn' [*Invitation to a Beheading*] (Paris: Dom Knigi, 1938, New York: Putnam, 1959, and London: Weidenfeld and Nicolson, 1960).

The Real Life of Sebastian Knight (Norfolk, Conn.: New Directions, 1941, and London: Editions Poetry, 1947).

Bend Sinister (New York, Henry Holt, 1947, and London: Weidenfeld and Nicolson, 1960).

Dar [*The Gift*] (New York: Chekhov, 1952, New York: Putnam, and London: Weidenfeld and Nicolson, 1963).

Lolita (Paris: Olympia, 1955, New York: Putnam, 1958, and London: Weidenfeld and Nicolson, 1959).

Pnin (Garden City, N.Y.: Doubleday, and London: Heinemann, 1957).

Pale Fire (New York: Putnam, and London: Weidenfeld and Nicolson, 1962).

Ada or Ardor: A Family Chronicle (New York: McGraw-Hill, and London: Weidenfeld and Nicolson, 1969).

Transparent Things (New York: McGraw-Hill, 1972, and London: Weidenfeld and Nicolson, 1973).

Look at the Harlequins! (New York: McGraw-Hill, 1974, and London: Weidenfeld and Nicolson, 1975).

Short Story Collections

Vozvrashchenie Chorba [*The Return of Chorb*] (Berlin: Slovo, 1929).
Nine Stories (Norfolk, Conn.: New Directions, 1947).
Vesna v Fial'te i drugie rasskazy [*Spring in Fialta and Other Stories*] (New York: Chekhov, 1956).
Nabokov's Dozen (Garden City, N.Y.: Doubleday, 1958, and London: Heinemann, 1959).
Nabokov's Quartet (New York: Phaedra, 1966, and London: Weidenfeld and Nicolson, 1967).
A Russian Beauty and Other Stories (New York: McGraw-Hill, and London: Weidenfeld and Nicolson, 1973).
Tyrants Destroyed and Other Stories (New York: McGraw-Hill, and London: Weidenfeld and Nicolson, 1975).
Details of a Sunset and Other Stories (New York: McGraw-Hill, and London: Weidenfeld and Nicolson, 1976).
The Enchanter [*Volshebnik*] (New York: Putnam, 1986).

Drama

Izobretenie Val'sa [*The Waltz Invention*] (New York: Phaedra, 1966, and London: Weidenfeld and Nicolson, 1967).
Lolita: A Screenplay (New York: McGraw-Hill, 1974).
The Man From the USSR and Other Plays (New York: Harcourt Brace Jovanovich/Bruccoli Clark, 1984, and London: Weidenfeld and Nicolson, 1985).

Verse

Stikhi [*Poems*] (Petrograd: privately printed, 1916).
Grozd' [*The Cluster*] (Berlin: Gamayun, 1922).
Gornyi Put' [*The Empyrean Path*] (Berlin: Grani, 1923).
Stikhotvoreniya 1929–1951 [*Poems 1929–1951*] (Paris: Rifma, 1952).
Poems (Garden City, N.Y.: Doubleday, 1959, and London: Weidenfeld and Nicolson, 1961).
Poems and Problems (New York McGraw-Hill, 1971, and London: Weidenfeld and Nicolson, 1972).
Stikhi [*Poems*] (Ann Arbor, Mich.: Ardis, 1979).

Translation

Anya v strane chudes [*Alice in Wonderland*] (Berlin: Gamayun, 1923).
A Hero of Our Time. A Novel by Mihail Lermontov (Garden City, N.Y.: Doubleday, 1958).

The Song of Igor's Campaign (New York: Random House, 1960, and London: Weidenfeld and Nicolson, 1961).
Eugene Onegin. A Novel in Verse by Aleksandr Pushkin (New York: Bollingen Foundation, and London: Routledge & Kegan Paul, 1964).

Prose

The Nabokov–Wilson Letters: Corresondence between Vladimir Nabokov and Edmund Wilson 1940–1971 (New York: Harper and Row, and London: Weidenfeld and Nicolson, 1979).
Lectures on Literature (New York: Harcourt Brace Jovanovich/Bruccoli Clark, 1980, and London: Weidenfeld and Nicolson, 1981).
Lectures on 'Ulysses' (Columbia, South Carolina: Bruccoli Clark, 1980).
Lectures on Russian Literature (New York: Harcourt Brace Jovanovich/Bruccoli Clark, 1981, and London: Weidenfeld and Nicolson, 1982).
Lectures on 'Don Quixote' (New York: Harcourt Brace Jovanovich/Bruccoli Clark, and London: Weidenfeld and Nicolson, 1983).
Perepiska s sestroy [*Correspondence with His Sister*] (Ann Arbor, Mich.: Ardis, 1985).
Vladimir Nabokov: Selected Letters 1940–1977 (New York: Harcourt Brace Jovanovich/Bruccoli Clark Layman, 1990).
Manuscripts: Berg Collection, New York Public Library.

Interviews

Breit, Harvey, 'Talk with Mr. Nabokov', *New York Times Book Review*, 1 July 1951, p. 17.
Clarke, Gerald, 'Checking in with Vladimir Nabokov', *Esquire*, July 1975, pp. 67–69, 131, 133.
Coleman, John, *The Spectator*, 6 November 1959, p. 619.
Davis, Douglas M., 'On the Banks of Lake Leman – Mr. Nabokov Reflects on 'Lolita' and 'Onegin', *National Observer*, 29 June 1964, p. 17.
Dommergues, Pierre, 'Entretien avec Vladimir Nabokov', *Les Langues Modernes*, January–February 1968, pp. 92–102.
Feifer, George, 'Vladimir Nabokov: An Interview', *Saturday Review*, 27 November 1976, pp. 20–26.
Gold, Herbert, 'The Artist in Pursuit of Butterflies', *The Saturday Evening Post*, 11 February 1967, pp. 81–85.
Hayman, John G., 'A Conversation with Vladimir Nabokov – with Digressions', *The Twentieth Century*, December 1959, pp. 444–50.
Jannoud, Claude, 'Vladimir Nabokov: le plus américain des écrivains russes', *Le Figaro Littéraire*, 13 January 1973, pp. 13, 16.
Lawrenson, Helen, 'The Man who Scandalized the World', *Esquire*, August 1960, pp. 70–73.
Levy, Alan, 'Understanding Vladimir Nabokov – A Red Autumn Leaf Is a Red Autumn Leaf, Not a Deflowered Numphet', *The New York Times Magazine*, 31 October 1971, pp. 20–22, 24, 28, 30, 32, 36, 38, 40–41.
MacGregor, Martha, 'The Author of "Lolita" – An Unhurried View', *New York Post*, 17 August 1958, p. M10.

Petchek, Willa, 'Nabokov Since Lolita', *The Observer*, 30 May 1976, pp. 15–19.
Sedykh, Andrey, 'U V.V. Sirina', *Poslednie Novosti*, 3 November 1932, p. 2.
Strong Opinions [22 interviews, 11 letters to editors, 14 articles] (New York: McGraw-Hill, 1973, London: Weidenfeld and Nicolson, 1974).
Wain, John, 'Small World of Vladimir Nabokov', *The Observer*, 1 November 1959, p. 21.

SECONDARY CRITICISM

Bibliography

Bryer, Jackson and Bergin, Thomas J., 'A Checklist of Nabokov Criticism in English', in Dembo (ed.), *Nabokov*, pp. 228–76.
Field, Andrew, *Nabokov: A Bibliography* (New York: McGraw-Hill, 1973).
Juliar, Michael, *Vladimir Nabokov: A Descriptive Bibliography* (New York: Garland, 1986).
Parker, Stephen Jan, 'Nabokov Bibliography', *The Nabokovian* [formerly *The Vladimir Nabokov Research Newsletter*], Annual Fall Issue, 1978– [bi-annual].
Schuman, Samuel, *Vladimir Nabokov: A Reference Guide* (Boston, Mass.: G.K. Hall, 1979).
Zimmer, Dieter E., *Vladimir Nabokov Bibliographie des Gesamtwerks* (Hamburg: Rowohlt Verlag, 1963).

Critical Studies

Alexandrov, Vladimir E., *Nabokov's Otherworld* (Princeton: Princeton University Press, 1991).
Appel, Alfred, Jr (ed.), *The Annotated 'Lolita'* (New York: McGraw-Hill, 1970).
Appel, Alfred, Jr, *Nabokov's Dark Cinema* (New York: Oxford University Press, 1974).
Appel, Alfred, Jr, and Charles Newman (eds), *Nabokov: Criticism, Reminiscences, Translations, and Tributes* (London: Weidenfeld and Nicolson, 1971).
Bader, Julia, *Crystal Land: Artifice in Nabokov's English Novels* (Berkeley, Calif.: University of California Press, 1972).
Barabtarlo, Gennady, *Phantom of Fact. A Guide to Nabokov's PNIN* (Ann Arbor, Mich.: Ardis, 1989).
Bloom, Harold (ed.), *Vladimir Nabokov* (Modern Critical Views) (New York: Chelsea House, 1987).
Bloom, Harold (ed.), *Vladimir Nabokov's 'LOLITA'* (Modern Critical Interpretations) (New York: Chelsea House, 1987).
Boyd, Brian, *Nabokov's 'Ada': The Place of Consciousness* (Ann Arbor, Mich.: Ardis, 1985).

Boyd, Brian, *Vladimir Nabokov: The Russian Years* (Princeton, N.J.: Princeton University Press, 1990).

Boyd, Brian, *Vladimir Nabokov: The American Years* (Princeton, N.J.: Princeton University Press, 1991).

Couturier, Maurice, *Nabokov* (Lausanne: Editions l'Age d'Homme, 1979).

Davydov, Sergey, *'Texty-Matreshki' Vladimira Nabokova* (Munich: Otto Sagner, 1882).

Dembo, L. S. (ed.), *Nabokov: The Man and His Work* (Madison, Wis.: University of Wisconsin Press, 1967).

Field, Andrew, *Nabokov: His Life in Art. A Critical Narrative* (London: Hodder and Stoughton, 1967).

Field, Andrew, *Nabokov: His Life in Part* (London: Hamish Hamilton, 1977).

Fowler, Douglas, *Reading Nabokov* (Ithaca, N.Y.: Cornell University Press, 1974).

Gibian, George and Stephen Jan Parker (eds), *The Achievements of Vladimir Nabokov: Essays, Studies, Reminiscences* (Ithaca, N.Y.: The Center for International Studies, Cornell University, 1985).

Grayson, Jane, *Nabokov Translated: A Comparison of Nabokov's Russian and English Prose* (Oxford: Oxford University Press, 1977).

Green, Geoffrey, *Freud and Nabokov* (Lincoln, Neb.: University of Nebraska Press, 1988).

Hyde, G. M., *Vladimir Nabokov: America's Russian Novelist* (London: Marion Boyars, 1977).

Johnson, D. Barton, *Worlds in Regression: Some Novels of Vladimir Nabokov* (Ann Arbor, Mich.: Ardis, 1985).

Lee, L. L., *Vladimir Nabokov* (Boston: G. K. Hall, 1976).

Meyer, Priscilla, *Find What the Sailor Has Hidden: Nabokov's 'Pale Fire'* (Middletown, Conn.: Wesleyan University Press, 1988).

Packman, David, *Vladimir Nabokov: The Structure of Literary Desire* (Columbia: University of Missouri Press, 1982).

Page, Norman (ed.), *Nabokov; The Critical Heritage* (London: Routledge & Kegan Paul, 1982).

Parker, Stephen Jan, *Understanding Vladimir Nabokov* (Columbia: University of South Carolina Press, 1987).

Pifer, Ellen, *Nabokov and the Novel* (Cambridge: Harvard University Press, 1980).

Proffer, Carl R. (ed.), *A Book of Things About Vladimir Nabokov* (Ann Arbor, Mich.: Ardis, 1974).

Quennell, Peter (ed.), *Vladimir Nabokov: A Tribute to His Life, His Work, His World* (London: Weidenfeld and Nicholson, 1979).

Rampton, David, *Vladimir Nabokov: A Critical Study of the Novels* (Cambridge: Cambridge University Press, 1984).

Rivers, J. E. and Charles Nicol (ed.), *Nabokov's Fifth Arc: Nabokov and Others on His Life's Work* (Austin, Texas: University of Texas Press, 1982).

Roth, Phyllis (ed.), *Critical Essays on Vladimir Nabokov* (Boston: G. K. Hall, 1984).

Rowe, William Woodin, *Nabokov's Spectral Dimension: The Other World in His Works* (Ann Arbor, Mich.: Ardis, 1981).

Shakhovskaia, Zinaida, *V poiskakh Nabokova* [*In Search of Nabokov*], (Paris: La Presse Libre, 1979).

Stuart, Dabney, *Nabokov: The Dimensions of Parody* (Baton Rouge, La.: Louisiana State University Press, 1978).

Tammi, Pekka, *Problems of Nabokov's Poetics: A Narratological Analysis* (Helsinki: Suomalainen tiedeakatemia, 1985).

Toker, Leona, *Nabokov: The Mystery of Literary Structures* (Ithaca, N.Y.: Cornell University Press, 1989).

Wood, Michael, *Vladimir Nabokov* (London: Routledge, Chapman and Hall, 1988).

Critical Articles and Chapters in Books

Alter, Robert, *Partial Magic: The Novel as a Self-Conscious Genre* (Berkeley: University of California Press), pp. 180–217.

Bell, Michael, '*Lolita* and Pure Art', *Essays in Criticism*, 24 (1974), pp. 169–84.

Delta 17 (October 1983) [Montpellier]. Nabokov Special Issue.

Dillard, R. H. W., 'Not Text but Texture: The Novels of Vladimir Nabokov', *Hollins Critic*, 3, 3 (June 1966), pp. 1–12.

Dolinin, A., 'Tsvetnaya spiral' Nabokova', in *Vladimir Nabokov. Rasskazy, 'Priglashenie na kazn', esse, interv'yu, retsenziy* (Moscow: Kniga, 1989), pp. 438–69.

Ermarth, Elizabeth, 'Conspicuous Construction: Or, Kristeva, Nabokov, and the Anti-Realist Critique', *Novel*, 21 (1988), pp. 330–39.

Erofeev, Viktor, 'Russkiy metaroman V. Nabokova, ili v poiskakh poterianogo raia', *Voprosy literatury*, 10 (1988), pp. 125–60.

Gerschenkron, Alexander, 'A Manufactured Monument?' *Modern Philology*, 63 (1966), pp. 336–47.

Grossmith, R., 'Spiritualizing the Circle: The Gnostic Subtext in Nabokov's *Invitation to a Beheading*', *Essays in Poetics*, 12, 2 (1987), pp. 51–74.

Hayles, N. Katherine, *The Cosmic Web: Scientific Field Models and Literary Strategies in the Twentieth Century* (Ithaca, N.Y.: Cornell University Press), pp. 111–37.

Johnson, D. Barton, 'The Books Reflected in Nabokov's *Eye*', *Slavic and East European Journal*, 29 (1985), pp. 393–404.

Josipovici, Gabriel. *The World and the Book: A Study of Modern Fiction*, 2nd ed. (London: Macmillan, 1979), pp. 201–20.

McCarthy, Mary, 'A Bolt from the Blue', *New Republic*, June 1962, pp. 21–27.

Modern Fiction Studies, 25, 3 (1979). Vladimir Nabokov Special Issue.

Rorty, Richard, *Contingency, Irony, and Solidarity* (Cambridge: Cambridge University Press, 1989), pp. 141–68.

Russian Literature Triquarterly. Special Nabokov Issue, 24 (1991).

Seidel, Michael, *Exile and the Narrative Imagination* (New Haven, Conn.: Yale University Press, 1986), pp. 164–96.

Tamir-Ghez, Nomi, 'The Art of Persuasion in Nabokov's *Lolita*', *Poetics Today: Theory and Analysis of Literature and Communication*, 1 (1979), pp. 65–83.

Tanner, Tony, *City of Words: American Fiction 1950–70* (London: Jonathan Cape, 1971), pp. 33–49.

The Nabokovian [formerly *The Vladimir Nabokov Research Newsletter*], ed. Stephen Jan Parker, 1978– [bi-annual].

Trilling, Lionel, 'The Last Lover', *Encounter*, 11 (October 1958), pp. 9–19.

Index